ECHOES OF
OLD CLYDE PADDLE-WHEELS

The Broomiela

Early Fifties

ECHOES OF OLD CLYDE PADDLE WHEELS

THE FIRST SIXTY YEARS
FROM THE COMET OF 1812

by
ANDREW McQUEEN

STRONG OAK PRESS

ISBN: 1-871048-25-7

Publishing history: This work was first issued in 1924 as a supplement and
companion volume to the author's CLYDE RIVER STEAMERS, published
1923. The original text and illustrations are reproduced here complete and
unabridged.

Published by   The Strong Oak Press
                      PO Box 47
                      Stevenage
                      Herts SG2 8UH, UK

Printed in Great Britain by Triographics, Knebworth, Herts SG3 6EX

PREFACE

THE reception accorded locally to my *Clyde River-Steamers of the Last Fifty Years*, and the numerous letters received from overseas, have shown the great interest taken by Glasgow men at home and abroad in the history of the river-fleet. The study of any history usually leaves the student desirous to know " What happened before that ? " and it is in the belief that such a desire may exist among readers of *Clyde River-Steamers* that the present volume has been written. Unlike its predecessor, it deals with a period outwith my own recollection, but with which careful study of contemporary records has made me conversant.

In these twenty-one sketches no attempt has been made to present a continuous narrative, but they treat of what, to my thinking, are the most interesting incidents in the first sixty years of the Clyde steamboats.

The chapter on " The First Sunday-Breaker " and the description of the " Plover " explosion, from "Old Clyde Tragedies," appeared last year in the *Glasgow Weekly Herald*; " By Heid-Mark " was published in the *Evening Times* some years ago, and part of " To the Coast in pre-Comet Times " in the *Evening News* more recently.

None of the other chapters has been printed before.

The frontispiece is of peculiar interest. The original photograph, taken by Mr. John Kibble, is the property of the Glasgow Corporation, to whom he presented it, and I am indebted to the courtesy of the Parks and Galleries Committee for permission to reproduce it. Dating as it does from the early 'fifties, it must be among the earliest photographs of its kind, and it is scarcely surprising that I have, so far, been unable to find anyone who can name the boats with any certainty. I shall be grateful to any reader who can do so, as it would add greatly to the interest of the photograph.

I have to thank all those who have supplied me with material for illustrations, and in a particular degree Mr. Richard Hubbard, who very kindly placed at my disposal his unique collection of contemporary drawings, including a number of boats of which no photographs exist.

ANDREW McQUEEN.

SHAWLANDS,
GLASGOW, *July* 1924.

SUPPLEMENTARY TO PREFACE

SINCE the foregoing was written I have been favoured with the views of several gentlemen whose recollections go back approximately to the date of the old Broomielaw photograph. Sifting

the evidence, I have come to the following
conclusions :—

The two boats with double-banded funnels, on
extreme left, belong probably to the McKellar
fleet, although one of them may be the Lochgoilhead boat. The black-funnelled boat to the right
of these is one of the Lochgoilhead steamers, the
" Sovereign " or " Monarch." The steamer
with two thin funnels, half black and half white,
is undoubtedly the first " Chancellor," the
Arrochar boat.

The next steamer, with two black funnels,
white-banded, is probably the " Petrel " in her
original two-funnel design, and in the Castle Co.'s
colours. It certainly is not the first " Eagle," as
suggested by some correspondents.

The steamer forward of this, with white funnel,
black-topped, is one of the Kilmun boats ; likely
the " Eclipse."

Ahead of her with single funnel, coloured like
those of the " Chancellor," is the Dumbarton
steamer, " Premier " or " Queen."

On the south-side are two of the Castle Co.'s
boats wearing black funnels with white bands.
The steamer with two white funnels has baffled
recognition so far.

I thank most heartily those gentlemen who
have so kindly given their assistance in the
identification.

ANDREW McQUEEN.

SHAWLANDS, *Sept.* 1924.

CONTENTS

PAGE

I. To the Coast in Pre-Comet Times - 1

II. In the Beginning - - - - - 7

III. Early Developments - - - - 15

IV. Old Clyde Tragedies - - - - 27

V. Some Steamboat Excursions of Long Ago - - - - - - - 37

VI. An Exchange of Compliments - - 45

VII. A River Greyhound of the Fifties - 55

VIII. The First Clyde Sunday-Breaker - 61

IX. A Box o' Tricks - - - - - 69

X. Lost by Stranding - - - - 75

XI. In Bowling Bay - - - - - 81

XII. The Upper Navigation - - - 87

XIII. Speed *versus* Comfort - - - - 95

XIV. The Eventful Voyage of the " Petrel " 103

XV. Record-Makers of the Rothesay Route 109

PAGE

XVI. THE PALMY DAYS OF RACING - - 119

XVII. THE PURCHASES OF THE " EMPEROR OF
CHINA " - - - - - - 129

XVIII. THE EARLY DAYS OF THE WEMYSS BAY
ROUTE - - - - - - - 145

XIX. IN THE OUTER WATERS - - - - 155

XX. THE ROCKY ROAD TO DUBLIN - - 163

XXI. BY HEID-MARK - - - - - 171

APPENDIX - - - - - - 177

LIST OF ILLUSTRATIONS

1.	THE BROOMIELAW IN THE EARLY FIFTIES	*Frontispiece*
		Page
2.	"COMET"	1
3.	REMAINS OF "INDUSTRY"	16
4.	A STEAMER OF 1817	17
5.	"SHANDON"	26
6.	"SUPERB"	27
7.	"LADY BRISBANE"	46
8.	"PIONEER"	47
9.	"GLENGARRY"	58
10.	"ENGINEER"	59
11.	"MARS"	78
12.	"PETREL"	80
13.	"GLENCOE"	81
14.	CROSS-HEAD OF "GLENCOE'S" STEEPLE ENGINE	88
15.	GILT ORNAMENT ON COMPANION OF "GLENCOE"	89
16.	"CYGNET"	100
17.	"MOUNTAINEER"	109
18.	"EAGLE"	113
19.	"VENUS"	120
20.	"WELLINGTON"	121
21.	"BARON"	128
22.	"LYNX"	129
23.	"IONA" No. 1	136
24.	"GAIRLOCHY"	137
25.	"NEPTUNE"	142
26.	"VICTORY"	152
27.	"LARGS"	153
28.	"BUTE"	161
29.	"MARCHIONESS OF LORNE"	168
30.	BOWLING BAY IN 1923	169
31.	A CORNER OF BOWLING BAY IN 1923	176

"Comet" (*built 1812*)

The ..... & Pioneer of Steam Navigation."

TO THE COAST IN PRE-"COMET" TIMES

In these present times of regular and frequent railway and steamboat communication to all parts of the Clyde coast it is hard to realise the state of affairs that existed in times before the paddles of the first steamboat had ruffled the surface of the Clyde, when muscle of horse and man were the sole motive powers available for land journeyings, and when water transit depended entirely on fickle wind or lab'ring oar. Instead of a rapid succession of trains to Greenock and Gourock, there were then but two conveyances daily. One of these was a mail-coach which carried but a few passengers, persons, no doubt, on business of urgency. Others, whose affairs admitted of more leisurely travelling, found accommodation in the "Royal George," a more commodious vehicle, with seats running lengthwise, after the style of the old city omnibuses, still within the recollection of elderly people. The "Royal George" was more cramped in its proportions than the omnibuses, however; it was set on six low wheels and drawn by as many horses, and was a much slower means of travelling than the mail-coach.

On the north side of the river, a one-horse caravan, or covered waggon, left Glasgow in

A

the early hours of the morning for Helensburgh. The journey occupied the whole day, and on reaching Bowling Bay a prolonged stoppage was made for dinner. This conveyance is said to have been much patronised by ladies and children.

Gentlemen, doubtless, rode, and as for the common people—well, they were a stay-at-home race, never venturing far afield, and the few who found occasion to make so long a journey most likely did it in leisurely fashion on "Shanks's nagie."

Those travellers who preferred to make the journey by water had the option, during the summer months, of embarking in boats seated for passengers, and rather inappropriately designated "fly-boats." Their progress was governed by the state of wind and tide, but except under the most favourable conditions their passages to Greenock or Gourock were not likely to be made under twelve hours. It was a frequent occurrence for these boats to take the ground anywhere between Renfrew and Dumbarton, and when that happened the crews were prone to scramble ashore and seek refreshment at the nearest hostelry until such time as the tide had made sufficiently to enable the boat to be refloated. The boat and passengers were left to take care of themselves in the interval, the crews knowing well that they were not likely to stray far or come to much harm.

For the truth of the following story, told of one

of these fly-boats, we will not vouch. It was late in the evening and quite dark, and the tide having reached full flood, the boat was ready to start from the Broomielaw. There was no wind, so the oars were resorted to, to assist the ebb-tide in carrying her down. The river and harbour were not lighted in those days, and the skipper at the tiller peered earnestly into the darkness for some landmark that might indicate the vessel's position. At length, as the first indications of dawn appeared, his eagle eye seemed to descry a familiar outline. "Noo, Tonal," he shouted, "shust give her some draws more; there's the Dumbarton Castle; she'll soon be at Greenock noo." The increasing daylight soon showed that the skipper's eyes had deceived him, and that the vessel, strange to relate, was still at the Broomielaw. An investigation into the cause of this phenomenon disclosed that, as the skipper expressed it, "She had been rowin' a' nicht wi' thon boo'd airn thing in"—in other words, they had forgotten to raise the anchor before starting to row.

Passengers for Dunoon and the Holy Loch had to make their way as best they could from Greenock or Gourock to the Cloch, and embark there in open boats, while those for Rothesay went on board small sailing packets at Greenock, and might be several days in reaching their destination. But there was very little traffic beyond Gourock or Helensburgh; these were the favourite watering-places for well-to-do people of the period, and a trip to Rothesay was looked upon in much the same light as an ocean voyage nowadays.

In *Glasgow Past and Present* Senex has given us very interesting descriptions of three separate journeys to the coast in the latter part of the eighteenth century. The first of these was made in 1778 to Rothesay, passage being taken in a small half-decked wherry which was loading for that port at the Broomielaw, and in which the family embarked with all their household plenishing, even to carpets, besides good store of bere-meal and sea-biscuit, for at the time there was not a baker's shop in the whole island of Bute. The vessel made a fine passage of something less than twenty-four hours, reaching Rothesay at three o'clock in the morning. Senex describes the Rothesay of the period as a fishing village of some 1500 inhabitants, mostly well-to-do people, owners or part-owners of herring-busses. There Senex with his mother and his brothers and sisters spent the season, his father making occasional visits, travelling by coach to Greenock and spending the night there before embarking.

In the following year the family took their holiday at Dunoon, then a mere Highland clachan. There were no vessels trading thither from the Broomielaw, so that a wherry had to be specially hired. The vessel stuck on a sandbank below Dumbarton and remained there several hours, but notwithstanding this reached Dunoon the same evening. The shores at that time, from the Holy

Loch right round to Toward, were in a state of
nature, and numerous seals were to be seen on
the rocks. The only road in the district led over
to Otter Ferry, on Loch Fyne side, and was used
principally by farmers and drovers. Both in
Rothesay and Dunoon Gaelic was the common
language.

Senex's third trip was to Largs in the summer
of 1782, that village having been chosen on
account of its accessibility by road, whereby the
tedium of a long sail could be avoided. A caravan
was hired for the journey, but the change could
hardly be regarded as a success, as on arrival at
Kilbirnie it was learned that the road, if such it
could be called, beyond that point was quite im-
passable for such a vehicle. The night had, consequently, to be passed at Kilbirnie, and in the
morning a couple of country carts were hired, to
which passengers and luggage were transferred,
but even these had considerable difficulty in
negotiating the rough and hilly path to Largs.
The head of the family, on his visits, took coach
to Greenock, where he hired a horse, and rode
the rest of the way, a boy being sent from
Greenock on foot to take the animal back. Largs,
although not yet a resort for summer visitors,
appears to have been a place of some commercial
importance, being the great centre of the cattle
trade between the Highlands and Lowlands; and
we are told that on the day of St. Colm's Fair at
least 400 vessels (doubtless very small ones) were

lying either at anchor in the bay or drawn up on the beach, while more cattle were to be seen than at a Glasgow Fair of the same period.

The experiences of the outward journey determined the family to make the return trip by sea, so at the close of their sojourn the Largs packet was chartered, and performed her part with great success, passengers and luggage being landed at the Broomielaw after a pleasant and extraordinarily rapid passage of twelve hours.

IN THE BEGINNING

ALL European steamships trace their descent from Henry Bell's " Comet " as their common ancestor. Nevertheless it is a mistake, though a common one, to describe Bell as the inventor of the steamboat. Steamboats were in existence long before the " Comet " appeared, and all that can be claimed for her is that she was the first steamer in Europe to ply regularly with passengers and to sail in open waters. It is not possible to say with exactitude who the inventor was, for the steamboat was rather a growth than an invention; the process was a very gradual one, for even so long ago as the sixteenth century men were exercising their ingenuity over the question of propelling vessels by steam. Many a forgotten experimenter, centuries before Bell, had devoted his life to the problem and died with it still unsolved, but perhaps leaving behind him as the result of his labours some contribution to the slowly-accumulating store of knowledge, a hint of something to be aimed at or avoided, which might guide a later investigator a little further on the long road to success. Doubtless the search had its toll of martyrs, too obscure for enrolment, who lost eyesight and even life itself through some unlooked-

for outbreak of the unruly force they vainly sought
to control. From the oblivion that surrounds these
early seekers after knowledge a few names have
been rescued, and in some instances extravagant
claims have been put forward for them which
careful sifting of evidence has either failed to
substantiate or entirely disproved.

Thus there was published in 1825 by a Spaniard
named Thomas Gonzalez a circumstantial account
of a steam-vessel, constructed by one Blasco de
Garay in 1543, and tried with success in the
harbour of Barcelona. Gonzalez asserted that
irrefutable proof of the story was contained in
documents preserved among the Royal Archives
of Spain at Simancas, in Catalonia, but not accessible to examination. More than thirty years later
Mr. John M'Gregor was allowed, through the
courtesy of the Spanish Government, to examine
the documents, but found that the vessel experimented with was not a steamer at all, but simply
a paddle-boat worked by man-power.

A Frenchman, Denis Papin by name, was
probably the constructor of the first actual steamboat. From letters of his, which have come to
light, it appears that he navigated a steam-propelled
vessel from Cassel to Munden, on the Fulda, in
1707; but the boatmen of the latter place, fearful
of the consequences to their trade, made a mur-
derous attack on him. The navigator escaped with
difficulty, but his boat fell a victim to industrial
intolerance. Papin is said to have found his way

to London, and died there three years later without having amassed funds to resume his experiments.

Jonathan Hulls, son of a Gloucester mechanic, took out a patent for a steam-propelled vessel in 1736, and published a descriptive pamphlet. His idea appears to have been to use his steamer for towing purposes only, but there does not seem to be any evidence that his invention ever took concrete form.

But the first steamboat applied to commercial purposes was undoubtedly that of John Fitch, which was placed on the Delaware in 1790. Newspaper advertisements of her sailings are still extant. "The Steamboat" (no name was required, as she was the only steamboat in the world) was announced to sail on 27th July from Philadelphia for Burlington, Bristol, Bordentown and Trenton, returning next day. Fitch, for some reason, distrusted paddle-wheels, and his boat was propelled by three or four broad-bladed oars at the stern, worked by an engine. She made a number of trips but was found unsatisfactory, as her machinery was very unreliable and was always getting out of order. Fitch was undoubtedly a genius; but his optimism was his undoing. Without funds himself, he had, of course, to borrow money for his projects, but invariably underestimated the cost of carrying them out. Usually, too, some improvements suggested themselves to him, involving extra expense, and further borrowings were rendered necessary, till the lenders, tired of looking in vain for some tangible result, withdrew their support. Unable to continue his experiments for lack of financial assistance, Fitch grew despondent and ended by taking his own life.

Contemporary with Fitch were the experiments of Patrick Miller and William Symington in Scotland, first on Dalswinton Loch and afterwards on the Forth and Clyde Canal, which were attended with considerable success. Miller was a man of some means, who had made steam navigation his hobby; Symington was an engineering genius. Although the prospects were quite encouraging, for the boat attained a speed of six miles an hour on the canal, the cost of the experiments alarmed Miller and he took no further part in them. Symington secured a new patron in Lord Dundas, chairman of the Canal Company, who commissioned him to build a steam-vessel for towage work. This boat, the " Charlotte Dundas," was completed in 1802, and delighted her constructor and his patron. She was a stern-wheel steamer, the upper portion of the hull being carried right to the after-end of the paddle, thus protecting the paddle as well as giving extra deck-space. The engine bore strong testimony to the genius of its designer; it was a direct-acting horizontal, in which the reciprocal motion of the piston was simply and effectively transformed into a rotary one without the complicated system of levers, crossheads and rocking-shafts that distinguished the machinery of the " Comet " and her successors. But the

directors of the Canal Company, financially interested in the retention of horse-haulage, were
alarmed at this innovation which threatened to
supersede the horse; complaints were made,
probably on slight foundation, that the wash from
the steamer's wheel was injuring the banks, and
not even Lord Dundas's influence could avert
the order for her withdrawal. The "Charlotte
Dundas" was laid up, and never ran again; people
yet alive can recollect seeing her remains lying at
Bainsford. Symington must have been born under
an unlucky star. Fortune used him badly, bringing him repeatedly to the verge of success and then
suddenly deserting him. The Duke of Bridgewater took an interest in him and gave him a
commission to build half a dozen steamboats for
canal work in England, and it looked as if
Symington's fortune was made; but the nobleman's
untimely death caused the whole project to col-
lapse like a house of cards. It was a cruel blow
for Symington, whose labours had seemed so near
fruition, and who now found himself deserted and
impoverished. In despair he sought consolation
in the bottle, and although he lived many years
longer it was only to see others reap where he
had sown, and at his death, in 1831, he was in
very straitened circumstances.

When the "Charlotte Dundas" was running,
Symington had received a visit from an American
gentleman, Robert Fulton, who showed great
interest in his vessel. In 1807 this man placed

a steamboat, called the "Catherine" of Clermont (usually referred to as the "Clermont"), on the Hudson river between New York and Albany. It is doubtful if he availed himself to any extent of Symington's ideas, for neither in hull nor machinery did his boat bear much resemblance to the "Charlotte Dundas." The start of the "Clermont" was not too encouraging, but Fulton's perseverance at length made her a commercial success, and steamboats multiplied rapidly on American rivers.

It was not till 1812, five years after the appearance of the "Clermont," that Henry Bell's "Comet" was placed on the Clyde. During the preceding summer Bell, in co-operation with a Glasgow engineer named Thomson, had conducted a series of experiments with a small paddle-boat propelled by manual labour, but the results had been negligible. The "Comet" was a tiny craft, measuring only 40 feet by 10 feet, the hull constructed by John Wood of Port-Glasgow, the engine by John Robertson of Dempster Street, Glasgow, and the boiler by David Napier of Camlachie. The boiler and engine were placed amidships on opposite sides of the boat; aft of these was a small cabin, entered from the after-end, and fitted all round with presses and concealed beds. In front of these were plain deal seats, and in the centre of the apartment stood a plain deal table. Originally the steamer had four paddles, two on each side, with floats measuring 15 inches by 12 inches. The after pair of paddles proved quite ineffective, and after a short trial a single pair was fitted. The tall funnel was equipped with a yard on which a square sail could be hoisted, and the whole boat was brightly painted, having for her figurehead a lady garbed in all the colours of the rainbow.

The original advertisement of her sailings, dated 2nd August, 1812, sets forth that this handsome vessel, as she is described, sailing by the power of wind, air and steam, will leave the Broomielaw on Tuesdays, Thursdays and Saturdays, at midday or as soon thereafter as may answer from the state of the tide (the " Comet's " five-foot draught made this proviso necessary), and Greenock on Mondays, Wednesdays and Fridays, to suit the tide. Her maiden voyage from her birthplace at Port-Glasgow to the Broomielaw took place on 6th August, and according to the " Glasgow Courier " of 8th August she covered the distance in three and a half hours. Bell himself was on board, as was also John Robertson, the constructor of the engine. William M'Kenzie, formerly a schoolmaster at Helensburgh, acted as her skipper; Duncan M'Innes, described as a Highlandman, was pilot; a brother of Robertson's attended to the working of the engine, and had a fireman, whose name is not recorded, to assist him. William Douglas, afterwards commander of a steamer called the " Waverley," completed the crew. These appear to have been the only persons on board on the maiden run, but a day or so later the "Comet" sailed from the Broomielaw as a passenger steamer. A courageous few took passage by her, not without misgivings, and even by the time she reached Bowling in safety complete confidence had not been inspired in all, for two gentlemen left her there, preferring to walk the rest of the distance to Helensburgh rather than be involved in the explosion which they felt was inevitable. But the "Comet" steamed on; soon the rock of Dumbarton echoed the patter of the little shovel-floats, the plume of smoke from the funnel receded towards Newark Castle, heralding her approach to her birthplace at Port-Glasgow, where surely the shipyard workers gave her a cheer as she passed, and so to the Custom House Quay at Greenock, where she moored in good safety, her voyage successfully accomplished, and the era of the Clyde passenger steamboat fairly inaugurated.

EARLY DEVELOPMENTS

THE little "Comet" was not long suffered to enjoy a monopoly of the steam traffic on the river. Almost before the public had convinced themselves that it was safe to travel by her, rival steamers were being started in opposition. The first of these, the "Elizabeth," was launched in November, 1812, and placed on the station on the 9th of March following. She was a larger and more powerful boat than the "Comet," with an engine constructed by John Thomson, who had been associated with Bell in the hand-paddle experiments of 1811. She had two cabins, one forward and one abaft of the engine-house, and Mr. Thomson has left us an interesting description of their furnishing, showing how marked a contrast it presented to the plain deal benches and table with which the cabin of the pioneer vessel was fitted. The "Elizabeth's" after-cabin was 21 feet long, the breadth being 11 feet 3 inches at the forward and 9 feet 4 inches at the after end; it was seated all round, and the floor handsomely carpeted, while a sofa, covered in marone, occupied one end, giving the whole a warm and cheerful appearance. The height from floor to ceiling was 7 feet 4 inches, and six small windows on either

side, made to slide up and down like the windows
of a coach, admitted plenty of light and air. Each
of these was furnished with a marone curtain with
tasselled fringes and velvet cornices, with gold
ornaments, giving a very rich effect. Above the
sofa a large mirror was suspended, flanked by
book-shelves containing a selection of the best
authors "for the amusement and edification of
those who may avail themselves during the passage"; while other amusements (not defined) were
also to be had on board. The fore-cabin, Mr.
Thomson admits, was rather small, measuring only
11 feet 6 inches by 9 feet 6 inches, but although
less luxuriously furnished than the after-cabin, it
possessed the same lofty ceiling and the same type
of windows, and was a very comfortable place
either on a cold day or a warm one. The owners
of the "Elizabeth" were evidently determined to
spare no trouble or expense in order to secure the
traffic, and the manifold attractions of the new
boat must have influenced many of the travelling
public, now over their first timorousness regarding
steam propulsion, to make their journeys by her
rather than endure the discomforts of the coach,
for we learn that in that year the tolls on the
Glasgow and Greenock road let for £1400 less
than in the previous year. In 1813 other two
steamers appeared, the "Clyde" and the "Glasgow," and a detailed description of the former
has come down to us, which her builders, Messrs.
Wood, contributed to the "Glasgow Monthly

Remains of "Industry" (*built 1814*)

Photo. by Mr. T. Baird, Glasgow.

A Steamer of 1817

Phot. from a Print in Kelvingrove Art Galleries

Repository," and which appeared in the issue of September, 1813. The extreme length of the "Clyde" was 75 feet, the breadth 14 feet, and the height of her cabin from floor to ceiling 6 feet 6 inches. She was built very flat, and drew only from 33 to 36 inches of water. Her after-cabin was 20 feet long, and entered from the stern. Between this and the engine-room was a space of about 15 feet, allowed for goods. The engine, of 12 horse-power, took up 15 feet of the length, forward of which was the fore-cabin, 16 feet long, and entered from the side. The paddle-wheels were 9 feet in diameter and 4 feet in breadth, and each carried eight floats made of hammered iron, with a dip of 15 inches light, or 18 inches loaded. Along the outer edge of the wheels ran a platform with a rail, which extended right round the vessel, and was supported by timbers reaching down to the vessel's side. Her funnel was 25 feet high and could carry a square sail 22 feet broad. The joiner and carpenter work of the hull cost £650, and the engine, boiler, etc., £700. The vessel could carry some 250 passengers, and was worked by a crew of five men. Her daily consumpt was about 12 cwt. of coal, and her speed in calm weather from four to four and a half miles an hour, but against any considerable head breeze three miles was the utmost she could manage. She seems to have run as a consort to the "Elizabeth," each steamer making the double journey daily between Glasgow and Greenock, except in the height of

summer, when, if the weather was fair, three single
trips apiece were sometimes overtaken. The single
fares between Glasgow and Greenock were five
shillings in the after-cabin and half-a-crown in the
fore-cabin, against ten or twelve shillings charged
in the mail and stage coaches. Still, quite a number
of passengers remained faithful to the older form
of conveyance, alleging in explanation of their
preference that the noise and vibration (which
were, no doubt, considerable), coupled with " the
smell of the steam," rendered steamboat travelling
unpleasant to them.

Before leaving the subject of the " Glasgow
Monthly Repository," it is interesting to note that
the December number contains a communication
in the form of a letter, signed " A. C. R.," strongly
advocating the advantages of stern-wheelers over
side-paddle boats, but the view put forward did
not find favour, for not till fifty years afterwards
did the first and only stern-wheeler take her place
in the river fleet. The " Kilmun," which sailed
between Glasgow and Kilmun during the Glasgow
Fair week of 1863, was an experimental stern-
wheel boat of David Napier's, which had been
running for some years on the Severn. The short-
ness of her Clyde service indicates that she was
not a success in these waters, and she lay idle for
two years in Bowling Bay before finding a purchaser. In the sale advertisements it is claimed
that she had run from Kilmun to the Broomielaw
in one hour and 48 minutes, but it is hard to

believe that such a feat, if performed, could have escaped all other notice, at a period when the speed craze was at its zenith.

1814 brought the "Morning Star," the "Princess Charlotte," the "Duke of Argyll," the "Marjory" (afterwards sent to the Thames to inaugurate steam navigation on that river), the "Trusty" and the "Industry." The two last-named were cargo-boats, although the "Industry" is said to have been originally intended for a passenger-boat but only to have made a couple of trips as such. Most of the boats of that time were short-lived, for improvements in steamboat construction came so rapidly that vessels soon became antiquated, so that few remained in service more than a dozen, or fifteen years at most, and their frequent changes of name, of which no accurate record was kept, render the tracing of their history a matter of great difficulty. In both of these respects the "Industry" was an exception to the rule, for she remained under her original name in the Glasgow and Greenock trade for nearly sixty years. She was built of oak, at Fairlie, by William Fyfe, for a Mr. Cochrane, tanner in Glasgow, her dimensions being 66.9 feet by 14.7 feet by 8.1 feet. The original side-lever engine, by George Dobbie, of Tradeston, was removed in 1828 and replaced by a new one, constructed by Caird & Co. Along with the "Trusty" she went into the service of the Clyde Shipping Co., who employed her partly as a lighter and partly as a tug, the steamer proving herself well adapted for either purpose. A newspaper article, giving an account of her history, appeared in April, 1857. It is headed " The Oldest Steamer in the World," and mentions that the " Industry " had just reappeared after an extensive overhaul of hull and machinery, in the course of which she had been equipped with a folding funnel to enable her to berth above Glasgow Bridge. The article also mentions that her sister ship, the " Trusty," was by that time out of existence, but the belief is expressed that the " Industry " was still good for the work of a number of years. Not long after this the old steamer was sunk through striking a submerged rock near Renfrew, but was salved and survived to carry on her service for sixteen years longer. Then she was withdrawn from the station and moored in Bowling dock, never, as it proved, to resume sailing, for she lay there till her timbers rotted. The engine, although in very bad condition from long exposure to the weather, was removed, and measures taken for its preservation as a relic of early marine engineering.

1815 produced the " Britannia," the " Dumbarton Castle," the " Caledonia," the " Greenock " and the " Argyll," bigger boats than their predecessors, averaging about 90 feet long; and in the following year there was quite a large crop of new boats, of which the most noteworthy were the " Rothesay Castle," the " Albion " and the " Marion." By this time the steamboat had fared

forth far beyond the narrow limits of the
" Comet's " original voyagings, and Gourock,
Largs, Dunoon, Rothesay, and even Campbeltown
and Inveraray were enjoying the advantages of
the new method of travelling, the last-named town
being brought within eighteen hours of Glasgow.

Bell, finding his poor little " Comet " elbowed
out of the trade by all these newcomers, sent her
to the Firth of Forth, via the canal, with the
intention of transferring her to the Thames, but
in the open waters outside of the firth the feckless
little engine proved quite helpless, and the
" Comet " was brought back to the Clyde. Attain-
ing no great success, she was again transferred to
the Forth to ply there, but with no better
results, so Bell brought her home again, had her
lengthened by 20 feet, and fitted with a more
powerful engine, and, greatly daring, placed her
in 1819 on the station between Glasgow and Fort-
William, by way of the Crinan Canal.

In the West Highland districts, where hitherto
the steamboat had not penetrated, the " Comet's "
appearance produced consternation; the inhabitants fled at her approach, or, concealing themselves, viewed with terror the uncanny stranger,
superstition proclaiming her some emissary of the
Powers of Darkness. The " Comet's " career on
the Fort-William route was but short, for on a
homeward trip in 1820, in stormy weather, lack
of engine-power rendered her unable to withstand
the Atlantic current, and she was driven ashore

near Craignish. The vessel broke in two at the point where she had been lengthened, but fortunately the portion on which the crew and passengers, including Bell himself, had collected, held fast, and all were rescued. The engine was recovered, and eventually presented to South Kensington Museum. It is interesting to note that the original engine, discarded when the vessel was lengthened, and which had cost £160 when new, was sold to a firm of coachbuilders in Miller Street, who used it for a considerable time in driving turning-lathes, and latterly sold it for £60. It changed hands several times afterwards, and was shown at an exhibition held in Messrs. Wylie & Lochhead's premises in Argyle Street in September, 1857. While it was there the place was destroyed by fire; probably the cylinder now in the Art Galleries at Kelvingrove represents all of the engine that it was found possible to rescue.

Of the boats of 1815, the " Caledonia," distinguished for the lavish gilt decoration of her stern, and the " Argyll " were sent to the Thames. The " Rothesay Castle " of 1816 was sold to Liverpool, and is best remembered for her disastrous end. On 17th August, 1831, she left Liverpool at eleven o'clock in the forenoon, well filled with passengers, on an excursion to Beaumaris. The weather grew bad, and with a skipper unfortunately not in a condition to navigate her, the steamer was driven on the Dutchman's Bank, near Great Orme's Head, where she was soon battered to pieces, with a loss of about a hundred lives.

The " Marion," built in the same year as the " Rothesay Castle," ran for a season on the river, and was then transferred to Loch Lomond, being the first steamboat to ply on that lake.

1817 produced but two boats, the " Duke of Wellington " and the " Defiance," the latter a small steamer, only 55 feet long, which appears to have been the pioneer of the Loch Goil route. In the following year the " Oscar," built at Dundee in 1814, and engined by Robertson, the same who had constructed the original engine of the " Comet," was brought round to the Clyde, and took her place on the Loch Goil station. Five new steamers made their appearance in this year, the " Marquis of Bute," the " Woodford," the " Active," the " Dispatch " and the " Rob Roy." The " Active " and " Dispatch " were cargo-boats, built to oppose the " Trusty " and " Industry " in the Glasgow and Greenock trade.

The " Rob Roy " deserves more than passing notice. She was built by Denny of Dumbarton to the order and design of David Napier, who constructed the engine for her at his own works at Camlachie. The steamers built up till then had been designed only for plying in smooth water, and to adapt hull and machinery to the comparatively stormy channel passages presented difficulties which Napier set himself to overcome. The story is well known how he took passage during a stormy

season, in one of the sailing packets then plying
between Glasgow and Belfast, and stood at the
bow, watching the action of the waves, going aft
once in a while to inquire of the captain if the
weather could be considered exceptionally rough,
and on receiving an answer in the negative returning to his post of observation. How, latterly,
the storm having greatly increased, and his inquiry
bringing forth the captain's admission that he had
seldom, if ever, seen a worse sea, Napier went
below satisfied, remarking, " I think I can manage,
if that be a'." And how, having carried out a
series of experiments with models on the Camlachie Burn, with a rough and ready contrivance
for measuring resistance, he designed the " Rob
Roy " in conformity with the results, and placed
her in the Glasgow and Belfast trade, the first
regular sea-going steamship in the world. Her
success attracted the attention of the French
Government, who bought her, and as the " Henri
IV." she was the pioneer mail steamer between
Dover and Calais.

The owners of the " Britannia," which had been
built for the Campbeltown station in 1815, sent
their vessel on an excursion to the Giant's Causeway and Londonderry, with such satisfactory
results that a regular service to Londonderry was
inaugurated with her, in which she was constantly
employed until wrecked in 1829.

In 1819 the " Robert Bruce " was built for a
company of Glasgow gentlemen, by whom she was

placed in the Liverpool trade; the " Robert Burns " was started between Glasgow and Ayr, and two other steamers, the " Fingal " and the " Samson," made their appearance. The first " Inveraray Castle," which took her place on the Loch Fyne station in 1820, was the largest and most powerful steamer then plying on the firth. The " Post-Boy," of the same year, was built for one of David Napier's enterprises. Owing to her shallow draught of 3 feet, she was able to leave the Broomielaw at a fixed hour, regardless of the state of the tide, and six o'clock each morning saw her depart for Dumbarton, whence passengers were conveyed by coaches to join the steamer " Marion " on Loch Lomond. The " Marion " returned from her cruise in time for passengers to join the " Post-Boy " at six o'clock in the evening for the upward journey.

Lumsden's " Steamboat Companion " for 1820 gives a list of 23 steamers plying from the Broomielaw. Of these, 17 traded to ports on the river and firth, 1 to Fort-William, 3 to Liverpool, and 2 to Belfast; surely a marvellously rapid development in the eight years that had elapsed since the little " Comet " ventured timorously forth on her first passage to Greenock.

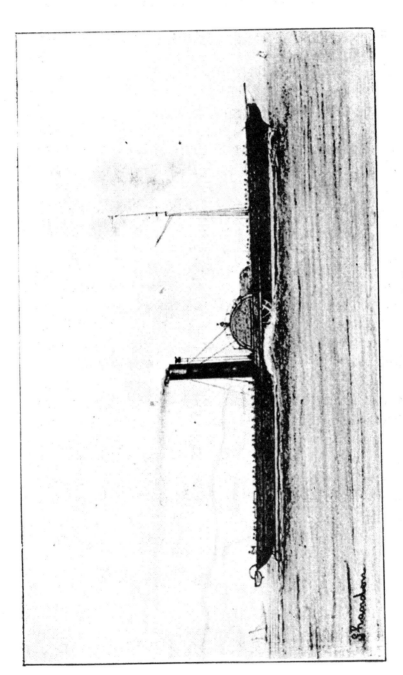

"Shandon" *(built 1837)*

Photo. from a Drawing in Mr. Hubbard's Collection.

"Superb" (*built 1839*)

OLD CLYDE TRAGEDIES

ALTHOUGH the Clyde river-service since its incep-
tion has been, as a whole, remarkably free from
serious disaster, the last sixty years showing an
immunity that might well be described as mar-
vellous, yet the earlier years are not altogether
without their catastrophes involving deplorable loss
of life. That such should occur was inevitable,
before legislation had devised rules for controlling
the construction and navigation of steamboats,
when boilermaking was in the experimental stage,
and when the rule of the road was elastic and the
carrying of lights at night optional. Indeed, it
says much alike for the skill and the conscientious-
ness of the early builders and skippers, fettered
by no restrictions save such as their own good
sense imposed, that this liberty was so little abused,
and that for nearly fourteen years from its beginning the history of the Clyde steamboat is not
marred by serious mishap. Then, however, came
an awful tragedy, by far the most appalling in the
record in respect to the destruction of life involved.
The victim was the second " Comet," a boat which
Henry Bell, with financial assistance from a number
of wealthy gentlemen, had built in 1821 to carry
on the Highland service after the wreck of his

original vessel. The second "Comet" was a much larger and more powerful boat than the first, far better fitted to face the weather to be expected on the station, and she appears to have plied with considerable success. The Caledonian Canal being opened in an unfinished condition in 1822 afforded a water passage to Inverness, and the steamer's journeys were prolonged to that town instead of terminating as they had formerly done at Fort-William. On the morning of 18th October, 1825, the "Comet" sailed from Inverness, arriving at Fort-William the same evening, her passengers disembarking there for the night. Next evening she reached Crinan, where the passengers were again put ashore, to rejoin the steamer the following morning. Owing to some unforeseen delay in the canal, Lochgilphead was not reached till ten o'clock, by which time the water was too low for the steamer to enter Loch Fyne, so that she was compelled to wait there until six o'clock in the evening. A detour to Rothesay for the purpose of obliging two passengers who wished to be landed there caused further delay, so that it was nearly two o'clock in the morning of the 21st when the steamer rounded the Cloch and stood up towards Gourock. The moon which had lighted her way up firth had now set, and the passengers, after a dance on deck, had nearly all gone below. The steamer was carrying no lights, and a jib which had been set interfered with the view ahead, so that the "Ayr" steamer, making her way down past Kempoch Point, neither saw nor was seen by the "Comet" in time to avoid a collision at full speed. The "Comet" immediately began to fill, and sank in three minutes, taking with her the majority of her passengers and crew. The "Ayr" at once put about and returned to Greenock without making any attempt to save the drowning victims, and her skipper has been much censured for his inhuman conduct, but, as his own steamer was only kept afloat with great difficulty and reached Greenock in a sinking condition, it is possible that his apparently cowardly action was the means of averting a greater loss of life. The death-roll was about seventy, the exact number never being ascertained, as no particular note had been kept of the passengers landing or embarking at intermediate ports. The hull of the "Comet" was afterwards raised, but found to be only fit for breaking up.

With the exception of the Campbeltown steamer "Kintyre," whose engineer was drowned when she was run down some fifteen years ago, the second "Comet" is the only vessel of the fleet whose loss by collision has involved any sacrifice of human life. The other steamboat tragedies have all been due to boiler explosions, for though strandings have been fairly numerous, and a few of the steamers have been lost thereby, no fatalities have resulted from them, while the few instances of fire on board have been equally innocuous.

The first boiler explosion occurred on board the

"Earl Grey" at Greenock Quay in 1835. The steamer, which was only three years old, was one of the biggest and finest on the river. Her short career had already been marked by misfortune, as in her first season she took fire in Brodick Bay one Sunday morning and sank in six fathoms. The accident at Greenock resulted in the death of ten persons, while fifteen more were severely injured, the vessel's decks being burst in all directions, exposing the cabin, into which a number of the boiler-tubes had been driven by the force of the explosion. The "Earl Grey" must have been repaired, however, as she is still advertised as sailing to Kilmun so late as 1842.

A steamer called the "Argyll," which plied to Inveraray, burst her boiler at Renfrew in 1839, one man being killed.

Even more destructive of human life than the "Earl Grey" disaster was the blowing-up of the "Telegraph" at Helensburgh quay in 1842. The "Telegraph" was a small steamer, of light construction, propelled by a locomotive engine working at high pressure, and was very fast. She had only been running for a few months, having taken up her station on 15th December, 1841. In an advertisement dated four days earlier, her owner expresses his confidence that the passage to Greenock will be made in 80 minutes, but owners in those days were prone to optimism with regard to the speed of new vessels. On the morning of 21st March, 1842, the "Telegraph" left the

Broomielaw at ten o'clock bound for Greenock, Helensburgh and Rosneath, and before noon she had landed her Greenock contingent, taken some others on board, and resumed her journey to Helensburgh. On her arrival there most of the passengers went ashore, and fortunately there were not very many on board when the order was given to start the engine. The paddles had only started to revolve when the boiler burst with a report that was heard for miles around, and fragments of the ill-fated steamer were flying in all directions. The death-roll was a heavy one, at least eighteen being killed on the spot, while several others afterwards succumbed to their injuries. Among those who lost their lives were Mr. Hedderwick, builder of the vessel, the captain, engineer, pilot and fireman, besides four out of a company of eight painters who were proceeding to the Gareloch to work on a new steamer lying there. Of the other four, two were severely and two slightly injured. The wonder is that any of those on board escaped with their lives, for the hull of the "Telegraph" was simply blown to matchwood, and of all the debris left floating not a single piece was more than a few feet in length. The wreck of the boiler and engine were blown shorewards and fell a considerable distance from the water, fortunately without injuring anyone in their descent. The exact cause of the explosion was never ascertained with certainty. The primitive safety-valves of those days were under the control of the engineer, who regulated the pressure by loading them with flat weights; probably the valve of the " Telegraph " was over-loaded. For some time after this disaster the Glasgow public were inclined to be distrustful of any vessel possessing more than the usual speed.

The last accident of this kind on the river took place at the Broomielaw on 5th February, 1851, two deaths resulting. A handsome little two-funnelled steamer called the " Plover," reckoned to be the fastest on the river, was lying at her berth that morning, due to start at half-past seven for Bowling, in connection with the Dumbarton-shire Railway. She had been built by Messrs. Wingate about two years before, and her steeple-engine of about 80 horse-power, together with her two haystack boilers, had been constructed from the designs of David Napier. Suddenly, a little after seven o'clock, a loud report echoed over a large portion of the city, and the dwellers in Carlton Place awoke from their slumbers and rubbed their sleepy eyes in alarm, wondering if a dreadful thunderbolt had expended itself over the city. The after-boiler of the " Plover " had ex-ploded, killing the engineer and terribly scalding two firemen, one of whom succumbed a day or two later in the infirmary. The force of the explosion was such that a piece of the outer covering of the boiler, measuring about 60 square feet, swept along the after-deck, clearing away everything in its path, including the companion and the funnel of the cabin stove, while a piece of metal weighing about a quarter of a hundred-weight was blown clean over some high houses on the north side of the river and fell in Ann Street, a hundred yards away. The dome of the boiler was blown to pieces, the funnel falling over the starboard side into the river and smashing the paddle-box in its descent. The steamer, in common with the other boats of the period, had no proper bridge, but simply a sort of gangway between the paddle-boxes, on which the steering-wheel was placed. This was smashed to pieces by the explosion and the wheel destroyed. The engine and the forward boiler are said to have escaped injury, but one is inclined to doubt this, as, although only two years old, the "Plover" was completely re-engined and re-boilered before she ran again.

Although, owing to the death of the engineer, it was not possible to get positive evidence of the circumstances attending the explosion, the cause seems obvious enough. It appears that the after-boiler had been emptied the previous evening, to receive some repairs, and after these had been effected water had been injected by means of a hand-pump. It is conjectured that the quantity thus put in had been insufficient to cover the top of the fire-box and tube-plate, which had consequently become red-hot, and that as soon as the donkey-engine was set to work to pump more water into the boiler steam had been generated so rapidly and in such volume that the safety-

valves, of which there were two, were quite
inadequate to give it egress, and the boiler itself
had to give way.

The " Plover " cannot be traced as having sailed
again on the Clyde, but in the advertising columns
of the newspapers, eighteen months after the
occurrence, we find offered for sale " the very fast
iron river-steamer ' Plover,' just refitted and furnished with entirely new engines and boilers."
The name of William Denny & Bros. appears at
the foot of the notice. A purchaser was found
in the Lancashire and Furness Railway, and the
steamer left her native waters to ply on the
Lancashire coast.

It would not have been surprising if this
accident had had an injurious effect on the
Broomielaw steamboat trade, or even if something
of a panic had ensued, but no such untoward consequences occurred. The Glasgow citizen of the
period was too fond of his sail " doon the watter "
to be deterred from it by anything so unlikely as
a boiler explosion; so much so that on the Spring
Fast-Day, just two months after the mishap, the
majority of the twenty-three steamers that sailed
on excursions from the Broomielaw had to put off
from the wharf, completely filled, before the advertised hour of sailing. Nor does any apprehension
appear to have been allowed to mar the joys of
the day's outing, as we learn from a contemporary
scribe that before Glasgow was reached on the
return journey " many of the male passengers had

become intoxicated " and that " only the strenuous exertions of police-officers and assistant harbour-masters averted a serious loss of life, for these not only prevented some people from falling into the river, but pulled others out after they had got in." Evidently, to anyone who took his holiday in such thorough fashion, the possible bursting of a boiler was but a minor risk.

The river-ferries too have their tale of fatalities, with which the river-steamers have been more or less connected. All of these occurred before the days of steam ferries, when the cross-river traffic was carried in row-boats. In 1834 a steamer called the " Kilmun " ran down the ferry-boat at Dun-glass and ten of the occupants were drowned. On 6th April, 1861, as the steamer " Lochgoil " was returning from Lochgoilhead, the Govan ferry-boat went alongside to take passengers ashore. It was a Saturday evening, and the steamer had a lot of excursionists on board, many of whom were more or less intoxicated. They crowded on board the ferry-boat in such numbers as to swamp her, and all were left struggling in the water; and although the majority got off with a ducking, the fatalities numbered half a dozen. Overcrowding, too, was the cause of the sinking of the ferry-boat at Clyde Street at the end of November, 1864. The boat left the ferry-steps loaded down almost to the gunwale just as the " Inveraray Castle " was passing. The steamer's paddles, which were of the old, non-feathering pattern, set up a considerable wash, which capsized the ferry-boat. The exact number of lives lost was never ascertained with absolute certainty, but it was not less than nineteen. The affair caused considerable sensation, and rules were established for restricting the number of passengers allowed on board the ferries, while at the same time the first steam ferry-boat, a vessel measuring 30 feet by 12 feet, was contracted for. The builders were Hedderwick & Co. of Govan, and the engine was constructed by Messrs. Howden. Less than a twelvemonth after the accident this little steamer was substituted for the row-boat at Clyde Street ferry.

SOME STEAMBOAT EXCURSIONS OF LONG AGO

THE steamboat in its earliest days was, no doubt, regarded merely as a rapid and comfortable means of conveyance between places at a distance from each other, but within a very short period its attractions for the holiday-maker were recognised. In Lumsden's " Steamboat Companion," published in 1820, there are described a large variety of excursions which the steamboat had brought within the reach of those on pleasure bent, but which, in earlier days, it would have entailed discomfort and hardship, with risk of much vexatious delay, to undertake. The island of Bute, the Sound of Kilbrannan, Loch Fyne, Loch Long, Loch Goil and Loch Lomond were all accessible to the holiday-maker with two or three days at his command, while those who could spare a week might visit the islands of the nearer Hebrides, the Giant's Causeway or the Isle of Man. Arran still remained difficult of access; no steamers plied thither, and the traveller who would visit it was counselled to take steamer to Rothesay and walk to the south end of Bute, where a boat of some sort might be found to convey him to the sister island.

Within the same year that produced Lumsden's " Companion " arrangements were made whereby the Glasgow excursionist could enjoy the delights of a cruise on Loch Lomond and return to the city in the course of a single day. The " Post-Boy " steamer, sailing from Glasgow at six o'clock in the morning, connected by means of coaches running between Dumbarton and Balloch with the " Marion " steamer plying on the Loch.

The " Marion " at that time had the whole expanse of Loch Lomond to herself, but ere long other steamers were placed on its waters, and on more than one occasion cut-throat competition took place. In such instances the rival steamers on the Loch made connection with different coaches, and these in their turn with different steamers on the Clyde. In 1844 the " Waterwitch " made her appearance on the Loch as a competitor of the steamer " Loch Lomond " then plying. The result was an immediate reduction of fares, and pas-sengers were carried from Balloch to the head of the Loch and back for a shilling in the cabin or sixpence in the steerage. As usual in such cases, the competition brought forth some exceptional specimens of the advertiser's art. One of these effusions was ostensibly by the steward of the new steamer. It runs thus :—

" D. M'Gregor most respectfully intimates to tourists and others that he has lately been appointed steward of that elegant and commodious steamer, the " Waterwitch," which has commenced plying for the season on Loch Lomond. D. M'Gregor trusts that from long experience, having held the situation of head waiter in one of the most respectable hotels in Glasgow, and from his determination to supply everything connected with the stewardship of the very best description and at the most moderate charges, to receive a share of the public patronage. From the saloon of this superior vessel being on deck, passengers are thus enabled to partake of breakfast, lunch, dinner, etc., at the same time enjoying the splendid scenery and admirable views of this celebrated loch."

In another notice attention is called to the fact that the " Waterwitch " proceeded right up to Inverarnan, enabling passengers to land at a newly constructed pier.

In the advertisements of the rival boat cold water is thrown on the Inverarnan part of the programme, and it is claimed as an advantage enjoyed by those who travelled by the " Loch Lomond " that they were not taken up the burn Falloch, " where there is nothing to be seen," and detained till the arrival of other conveyances from the north, but were carried directly up and down the lake. In one particular they were more favoured than the tourists of the present day, who may well envy them the privilege they enjoyed of landing on the downward journey on Inch Tavannach, the view from whose summit is described as perhaps not equalled and certainly not surpassed in Britain. " It embraces," says the advertiser, " about 120 square miles of lake scenery, spread out in every variety of strait,

creek and bay, interspersed with islands of every
shape and size, from Inch Galbraith, so small as
to be nearly covered by the ruins of the old castle,
to Inch Murrin, three miles in length and stocked
with several hundred head of deer, while Inch
Moan, scarcely elevated above the surface of the
water, with its crescent-shaped beach of pearly
whiteness, contrasts with that high and sombre
resting-place,

> 'Where deep pines on Inch Cailleach wave
> Their shadows o'er Clan Alpine's grave.'

"Directly to the west of this vantage-point,"
he tells us, "lies the hamlet of Altochlye, once
the scene of a bloody struggle between the
Colquhouns and the MacGregors; to the south-
ward lies the charming Vale of Leven with Dumbarton Castle and the hills of Renfrewshire in the
background; the east shows the termination of
the Grampian range, the Pass of Balmaha and the
village of Killin with George Buchanan's monu-
ment; while the view to the north is closed in
by such lofty mountains as Ben Voirlich, Ben
Duchray, Ben Loie and Ben Lomond." Another
of the attractions of the "Loch Lomond's" service to which attention is called in the advertisement was the option of going ashore at Tarbet,
whence Arrochar could be reached on foot in
ample time to catch the steamer and finish the
journey via Loch Long.

But in spite of these inducements to travel by

the " Loch Lomond," the " Waterwitch " survived her on the lake; probably the views obtainable through the cabin-windows of the latter, when accompanied by the catering of D. M'Gregor, were more to the public taste than any that could be got from the top of a hill. The description of the " Waterwitch " as having her saloons on deck is noteworthy, and if accurate would stamp her as having anticipated a style of construction which did not come into vogue for many years afterwards. A contemporary picture of her would be of great interest, but there does not appear to be one in existence. In her latter days, towards the close of the 'forties, the " Waterwitch " carried passengers to Inversnaid, for the steamer " Rob Roy " on Loch Katrine, bringing that lake also within the range of the daily tripper from Glasgow.

On the Firth some remarkable feats were accomplished in the matter of one-day trips. As a rule these entailed pretty early rising on the part of the traveller, five or even four o'clock in the morning being by no means unusual hours of starting, but the readiness with which people in these later days have adapted themselves to " Summer Time " proves that such early hours in the height of summer are no hardship.

In the same year that witnessed the appearance of the " Waterwitch " on Loch Lomond a company which had steamers plying to Largs and Millport arranged to place one of their boats in service between Ayr and Stranraer in connection with the railway from Glasgow to Ayr. The season was midsummer, and as the steamer destined for the new service was lying at Glasgow and had to be sent round to her station, advantage was taken of the occasion to arrange an attractive one-day trip from Glasgow. The steamer took her departure from the Broomielaw at four o'clock in the morning, steaming to Ayr and calling at Gourock, Largs and Ardrossan on the way. Those who found the early start from the Broomielaw a disadvantage were given the option of travelling by a train from Glasgow at half-past seven in the morning to Ayr and joining the steamer there. From Ayr the "Lady Brisbane" (that was the name of the steamer) proceeded to Girvan and thence to Ailsa Craig, where passengers were landed, the vessel remaining long enough to give them an opportunity of making their way to the top of the rock and back. The "Lady Brisbane's" return journey terminated at Ayr, which was reached in time for passengers to catch the seven o'clock train for Glasgow. In landing passengers on the Craig the owners of the "Lady Brisbane" displayed an enterprising spirit which has not been imitated by the excursion promoters of later days.

About seven weeks after this occasion, on the 8th of August, to be exact, a festival of the Grand Order of Modern Druids, held at Ayr, created so much interest in Glasgow that no fewer than three steamers were despatched in the early hours of the morning on special single-day excursions to the "Auld Toon"; the "Cardiff Castle" sailing at four o'clock, the "Superb" at 4.15, and the "Engineer" at 4.30. The first and last of these, which were new boats, carried excursionists at 4/- cabin or 3/- steerage for the return journey, but by the "Superb," an older boat, the fares were 3/- and 2/6 respectively.

But a more ambitious undertaking than any of these was advertised at the Glasgow Fair holidays of 1850, no less than a single-day excursion to Ireland and back. On 13th July, the Fair Saturday, a train was despatched from Bridge Street Station at half-past five in the morning for Ardrossan. There a very fine paddle-steamer, the "Firefly," one of the fastest then running in the channel trade, was waiting to convey passengers to Belfast. The "Firefly's" fourteen-mile gait enabled the voyage to be completed by one o'clock. After spending a couple of hours in the Emerald Isle the excursionists re-embarked for the homeward journey, and a very full day's outing ended at Bridge Street Station about eleven o'clock. The single-day excursion was not repeated in subsequent years, but it stands out as an extraordinary feat, rendered possible only by the "Firefly's" exceptional speed and the ability and energy which characterised the management of the Ardrossan-Belfast route more than seventy years ago.

AN EXCHANGE OF COMPLIMENTS

A paragraph appeared in the "Glasgow Herald" of 18th February, 1842, to the following effect:—

"We understand that a new iron steamer is in course of construction under the auspices of an influential company, for the Largs and Millport station. It is the intention of her owners to make her a first-class vessel, and she will open up a connection between these beautiful watering-places and this city. To the inhabitants of Largs and Millport a boat devoted specially to their accommodation must be a valuable acquisition, while a fast and commodiously fitted up vessel, sailing at positive hours and performing her voyages with regularity, must be highly desirable to visitors."

There were then two wooden steamers, the "Victor" and the "Warrior," maintaining the Largs and Millport service. They were owned by a company of Glasgow gentlemen, among whom was a Captain Duncan M'Kellar, who acted as managing owner and commanded one of the steamers. M'Kellar had served in the Army, and the martial style of nomenclature which the company adopted for their boats (their first had been the "Hero") was a recognition of the fact. In reading the "Herald's" paragraph one might

readily be misled into concluding that no daily
service between Glasgow, Largs and Millport was
then in existence, whereas each of the M'Kellar
boats made a daily trip during the summer, the
" Warrior " prolonging her voyage to Ardrossan
on three days of the week. There was no means,
however, of getting from the coast ports to Glasgow and returning the same day, until this was
provided by the new steamer. The " Lady Brisbane," as she was called, made her appearance in
July, just before the Fair holidays, and was advertised to leave Millport each morning at eight
o'clock and Largs at 8.45, and arrive at Greenock
in time for her passengers to catch the 10.30 train
for Glasgow. On the downward journey the
steamer was to leave the Broomielaw at 3.15, connecting at Greenock with the four o'clock train
from Glasgow. There was keen rivalry between
the two companies during July and August, for
the M'Kellar boats had enjoyed a monopoly of
the station for several years, and their owners
resented the intrusion of the " Lady Brisbane,"
and a certain amount of bitterness resulted, which
found its expression in print early in September.
Both companies had discovered, or had imagined,
that an idea had got abroad that the " Lady
Brisbane " was running in connection with the
M'Kellar boats, and the " Herald " of 5th 'September contains a disclaimer from each company.
The M'Kellar people contented themselves with
the bald statement :—" Observe ! No connection

Lady Brisbane

"Lady Brisbane" (*built 1842*)

"Pioneer" (*built 1844*)

Photo by Messrs. McIsaac & Riddle, Oban

with the ' Lady Brisbane ' steamer "—a declaration
to which, surely, no exception could be taken.
The new company, however, had a good deal more
to say on the subject. Not content with simply
disowning the supposed connection, they went on
to extol the excellence of their own boat and dis-
parage her rival. Their notice reads : " It having
been stated that the ' Lady Brisbane ' and ' Victor '
were connected, the proprietors beg to intimate
that such is not the case. The ' Lady Brisbane '
is a new, swift and first-class steamer, and the
' Victor ' an old one. The public are respectfully
informed that it is the intention of the proprietors
to start another new steamer as consort to the
' Lady Brisbane ' next season."
The allusion to the " Victor " as an old boat
is not in the best of taste, the more so as she
had only been running for some five years. It
was, doubtless, meant to irritate, and if so, it certainly succeeded, for the two companies were
speedily engaged in a wordy warfare, worthy of
the " Eatanswill Gazette " and " Eatanswill Inde-
pendent." The owners of the " old boat " found
a convenient weapon ready to hand, and did not
scruple to use it. The disastrous explosion of the
high-pressure steamer " Telegraph," a few months
before, had awakened in the public mind some
distrust of swift boats, so they proceeded to cast
doubts on the methods by which the rival steamer's
speed was attained. In the next issue of the
" Herald," on 9th September (the paper was only

published twice a week in those days), they inserted the following : —

" ' Victor.' No connection with the ' Lady Brisbane,' new steamer tho' she be, and the ' Victor ' an old one, as the opposition advertisement has it. As to being old, the ' Victor ' has certainly been on the station long enough to establish her character for SAFETY as well as SWIFT SAILING, and requires to use no extra or dangerous pressure for the latter purpose. Besides, not only another steamer, but TWO of them, IF REQUIRED, to ply as consorts to the ' Victor,' will be started in due season."

The owners of the " Lady Brisbane " must have had word of the contents of this notice before its appearance in the newspapers—probably it had been printed as a handbill or placard—for immediately below is found the following counterblast : —

" In consequence of the unfounded innuendo thrown out by the party connected with a rival steamer, regarding the speed of the ' Lady Brisbane,' and that she is sailed on an unsafe principle, the proprietors of that vessel consider it both due to themselves and the public safety to disabuse the public mind against the assertions which have been so liberally poured forth by their opponents, and in doing so, beg leave to say that a report has been drawn up to-day, but too late for publication, by two eminent engineers of this city, who have inspected the vessel, which will be made public at the earliest opportunity."

The report was duly printed in the issue of 12th September, and the public were invited to judge of it for themselves. It runs thus:—

"To the Managing Director of the 'Lady Brisbane' steamer. Sir: At your request we have examined the 'Lady Brisbane' steamer's boiler. We are certain that it is wrought on the low-pressure principle, and that she is perfectly safe with the pressure it is wrought with.—We are, Sir, Your Obedient Servants,

"DAVID SMITH
  "(of Smith & Rodger, Lancefield).
"WM. NAPIER (Washington Street)."

Evidently the "Lady Brisbane" people thought that this should silence their opponents, but instead of that it only furnished material for a fresh jibe, four days later, in the following terms:—

"In consequence of the well-known speed and safety of the fine steamer 'Victor,' unfounded insinuations have been thrown out against her by the party or 'managing partner' connected with a rival company, and a very silly announcement that theirs is a new steamer and the 'Victor' an old one. The proprietors of the 'Victor' have now to submit that any report on the subject (even by eminent engineers) is uncalled for, the Public having decided already, and by their decided preference and support declared that the 'Victor' is still at least equal to any boat on the station."

The "Lady Brisbane's" proprietors affected to

treat this effusion with disdain, their next effort
reading : —

"No connection with the 'Victor' steamer and
no attention paid hereafter to the attempted wit
of the 'managing partner tho' he be' of that
vessel."

The newspaper controversy lapsed until the
following year, when the "Lady Kelburne" joined
the "Lady Brisbane" on the station. Her trial
trip down the river was made the occasion for
much cheering and firing of guns. The enthusiasm
was not shared by the "Victor" people; it was
their turn to affect indifference, though at the same
time they deemed it wise to make arrangements
for placing a new iron steamer on the station in
the following summer and to advertise the fact.
When making the announcement they went on to
say : —

"In the meantime the 'Victor's' proprietors are
not at all apprehensive of not getting a full share
of the trade even in the face of the present grasp-
ing and barefaced attempt at monopoly by other
parties. This company never persecutes or annoys
passengers with personal solicitations or impor-
tunities to go by their boats,—never charges
higher fares than advertised,—and, above all, never
outrages public decency by publishing scurrilous
and disgusting placards in the silly attempt to dis-
parage other rival steamers. A specimen of such
dirty work, however, may be seen any day on
board the 'Victor.'"

In the summer of 1844 the new M'Kellar boat made her début. She was a very fast and very smart-looking steamer, built of iron, no expense being spared in her external and internal adornment, and the name " Invincible " was bestowed on her in token of her owner's confidence. In the same year the rival company added the " Countess of Eglinton " to their fleet, but her career was short, for after a few months' service she was put ashore on the Eilans and became a wreck. The " Mars," a similar steamer to the " Invincible," replaced the " Victor " in the following year, but the exchange of newspaper courtesies had ceased, and within a short time all the vessels were sailing under the M'Kellar houseflag. The addition of new vessels every other year gave an index to the prosperity which was attending the trade, and the sailings were extended to include Ayr and the Arran ports. In 1849 the " Star " came from Tod & M'Gregor's yard, and in 1852 the " Venus," a fine two-funnelled steamer, from J. & G. Thomson's. In 1853 John Barr built the " Vesta " to replace the " Invincible," which he probably took over in part payment, as his name appears as owner during the few years she remained on the Clyde. The " Mars " was lost by stranding in 1855, and in the following year the " Jupiter," built by Tod & M'Gregor, by far the biggest and finest steamer the company had owned, was placed on the Arran route. The " Juno," similar in design to the " Jupiter " but rather larger, which came

out in 1860, was the last vessel built for the
M'Kellar fleet. The owners realised that the opening of the Wemyss Bay route was bound to have
a prejudicial effect on the trade from the Broomielaw to Millport and Arran, so they took the
opportunity presented by the demand for blockade-
runners to get rid of three of their vessels—the
" Jupiter," " Juno " and " Star." About the same
time the " Vesta " was sold to a firm in the
Rothesay trade, so that the owners were left with
only the " Venus," " Lady Brisbane " and " Lady
Kelburne." A service was maintained up till the
end of 1867 season, when it lapsed and the boats
were put in the market. The " Lady Brisbane "
was bought at a low price by Hugh Keith in
March, 1868, for excursion work on the Firth.
The " Lady Kelburne " lay at Bowling till August,
1869, being then sold at scrap price, probably for
breaking up. The " Venus " was purchased by
her skipper, Captain Gillies, and plied for a few
years on the Wemyss Bay station before going
to the scrap-heap. The " Lady Brisbane," renamed
the " Balmoral," was running on the Foyle for a
short period in the autumn of 1869, but the next
season came back to the Clyde and was known as
a regular trader to Garelochhead for more than
twenty years, her hull serving for long afterwards
as a coal-hulk at Newry. The " Vesta's " career
lasted over thirty years altogether, her employment
during the last twenty being principally on the
Holy Loch and Gareloch stations. It ended with

an outbreak of fire at Ardnadam, which burned her to the water's edge. Of the three boats that went blockade-running, the "Jupiter" and the "Juno" had little luck, and the early capture of the one and foundering of the other must have rendered them very unprofitable speculations to their purchasers. The "Star," on the other hand, made a number of successful runs and managed to evade capture, remaining at Nassau after the war. She is still included in the latest issue of Lloyd's Register under her original name, now, at the ripe age of seventy-five years, the last survivor of the old M'Kellar fleet.

A RIVER GREYHOUND OF THE 'FIFTIES

It was just at the middle of the nineteenth century that Messrs. David Hutcheson & Co., the predecessors of the present firm of David MacBrayne, Ltd., took over the West Highland business of Messrs. G. & J. Burns and the vessels engaged in carrying it on. The tourist traffic must even then have been considerable, for the fleet comprised no less than eight vessels, all fitted for carrying passengers. Six of these were paddle-steamers, the remaining two being track-boats employed on the Crinan Canal. The " Pioneer " sailed daily during the season between Glasgow and Ardrishaig, leaving the Broomielaw at six o'clock in the morning, with a train connection to Greenock at seven, and returning from Ardrishaig at one o'clock in the afternoon. Passengers for the West Highlands travelled to Ardrishaig and thence by the track-boats " Sunbeam " and " Maid of Perth " to Crinan, whence the " Shandon " conveyed them to Oban. The " Dolphin," stationed at Oban, plied on Mondays, Wednesdays and Fridays through the Sound of Mull to Tobermory, and thence to Staffa and Iona. On Tuesdays, Thursdays and Saturdays her route was from Oban to Fort-William, connecting with the " Curlew," plying on the Caledonian Canal between Banavie and Inverness. The "Cygnet" and "Lapwing" traded between Glasgow and Inverness. These two were peculiar-looking boats, their dimensions being restricted to enable them to enter the locks on the Crinan Canal, through which their route lay. They were bluff-bowed, the stems being of a rounded form, with forecastles and poop-decks, which though small took up a good proportion of the entire length of the vessels, as they measured less than 90 feet over all. Each boat had two masts, and a tall funnel perched behind the paddles. The paddle-boxes were let in flush with the bulwarks, for convenient handling in the locks. These funny-looking little steamers must have been pretty lively in anything of a sea; much too lively, probably, for the comfort of the majority of the passengers.

The "Pioneer" was a good specimen of the better class of river-boats plying at the time, a commodious boat, flush-decked, as were all her contemporaries of the river-fleet, steeple-engined, and of a speed above the average.

The new firm were alive to the opportunities which the passenger trade afforded for development, and took energetic measures for its encouragement. During the Fair week of 1851 they advertised a series of cheap excursions in the second cabins of their steamers, " in order to afford the operative classes and others an opportunity of viewing the Western Highlands and Islands." The programme was as follows:—Leave Glasgow

Bridge at 6 a.m. for Ardrishaig, thence by track-boat to Crinan, and by steamer to Oban, arriving same evening. Leave Oban the following morning, sailing round Mull and visiting Staffa and Iona, reaching Oban again in the evening, and returning to Glasgow next day viâ Crinan and Ardrishaig. The fare for the three days' sailing was only 10/- for a single person or 12/6 for a married couple.

Good boat though the "Pioneer" was, Messrs. Hutcheson were convinced that the Ardrishaig trade afforded possibilities for something better, so they determined to transfer her in the following summer to the Crinan-Oban station, in lieu of the "Shandon," which was becoming rather antiquated, and to replace her on the Ardrishaig route by a new boat, which should surpass in speed and comfort any river-steamer afloat. The contract for the hull and engines was given to Messrs. J. & G. Thomson, whose Clyde Bank shipyard, then located at Govan, has bequeathed its name to a flourishing industrial town on Clydeside. From the Govan yard the new steamer was launched on 29th May, 1852, Master David Hutcheson, nephew of the owner, dressed in full Highland costume, naming her "Mountaineer" as she left the ways. Her trial-trip took place on 22nd July, and the results were eminently satisfactory. There was no measured mile at Skelmorlie in those days; the regular test for a new vessel was to "run the lights," i.e., from Cloch to Cumbrae, a distance of 15⅔ statute miles. This run the "Mountaineer " accomplished in $54\frac{1}{2}$ minutes, or at a speed of almost 15 knots, which, it was claimed, proved her to be the fastest steamer in European waters. Nor was speed her only distinction, for she was universally recognised as one of the handsomest vessels of her time, and many an admiring eye marked the gracefulness of her model and the easy flow of her lines. Her owners took great pride in her; to them she was much more than a mere item in a fleet; she was their crack boat, and as such was entitled to have much money lavished on her adornment. On either side of her bow was a finely carved and coloured representation of a Highlander in full costume, engaged in holding a greyhound in leash and apparently in stalking, while her stern bore similar figures in repose, with various implements of the chase designed in bas-relief between them. These decorations may be regarded as tributes to the excellence of the steamer herself, but the comfort of the passengers was not forgotten, as her internal adornment was on an equally lavish scale. On her flush after-deck was a spacious companion, oak-painted, and with a pane of stained glass, bearing a design of a mountaineer and his dog. The main-saloon, to which this companion-way gave entrance, had been furnished by Messrs. Boyd & Son, of Glasgow. It was a large apartment, surrounded by a richly-cushioned seat with carved rosewood back, and broad mirrors were placed at either end, which magnified its apparent size. But the most

"Glengarry" (*built 1844*)

Photo. by Messrs. G. W. Wilson & Co., Aberdeen (now Mr. Fred J. Hardie)

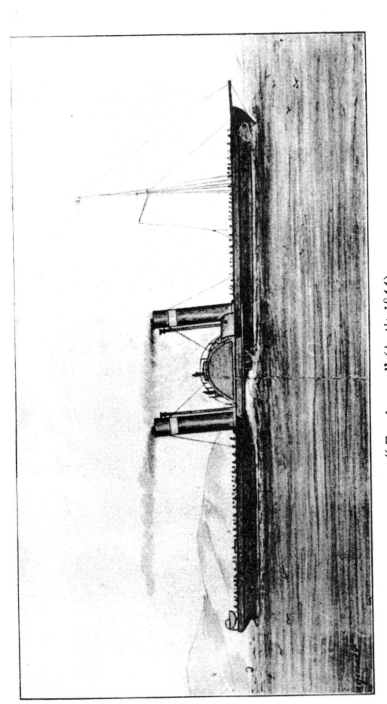

"Engineer" (*built 1844*)

Photo. from a Drawing in Mr. Hubbard's collection

striking feature in the decoration was a series of sixteen paintings on glass by Mr. T. Lawrie, of Glasgow, illustrative of Highland scenery, costumes and manners. Among the subjects were :— The Clyde from Dalnottar, Loch Oich, Inverlochy Castle, the Sound of Kerrera, the Falls of Foyers, Loch Leven, Linlithgow Palace, Dunolly Castle, the Trossachs, Loch Eil, Dunstaffnage, Loch Lomond, a Highland ferry, and Deerstalking; the subjects of the remaining two are not recorded. These were placed in the panels between the cabin windows, which themselves bore floral designs in stained glass. Additional light and ventilation were furnished to the saloon by a cupola of stained glass on the after-deck, a feature once universal on the Clyde boats, but which disappeared with the last of the flush-deckers. Altogether the " Mountaineer " was replete with every luxury of her time, and the prediction confidently made that she would promptly establish herself as a general favourite was amply verified.

Running the lights, in the summer of 1853, the " Mountaineer " reduced the time of her first trial by a minute, and altogether she acquitted herself admirably on the Ardrishaig route. But the trade developed so rapidly that ere she had been running three years a bigger and faster boat was called for, and in 1855 the " Mountaineer " resigned her station to the first " Iona " and was transferred to Oban. For many years she maintained the winter service on her original route, but it was in the outer waters that the old vessel met her fate. On the last run of the season, in September, 1889, her machinery broke down and she went ashore in the Sound of Mull. The hull was little damaged by the stranding, but before her salvage could be accomplished stormy weather set in and the old " Mountaineer " went to pieces. In her there perished perhaps the finest specimen of a river-boat of the early 'fifties.

THE FIRST CLYDE SUNDAY-BREAKER

QUITE a flutter agitated the watering-places of the Firth of Clyde when, in June, 1853, a rumour went round that a scheme was afoot for running a Sunday excursion steamer from the Broomielaw. Save that in the early 'twenties the Castle Company had been accustomed to despatch one of their steamers on a mail run from Rothesay to Greenock on the first day of the week, the Sabbath quiet of these resorts had so far remained undisturbed by paddle-beat. And now it was threatened, not by a comparatively respectable mail-boat, for which perhaps, if Sunday-breaking can under any circumstances be condoned, some extenuation might be found, but by a godless pleasure-steamer, whose passengers had come out with the deliberate intention of being "as happy as if it were the middle of the week." What wonder if the godly shuddered at the prospect and cast about them for some means whereby the threatened desecration might be averted! Rumour, ever a lying jade, connected the name of the "Reindeer" with the project, but the proprietors of that vessel promptly had an indignant disavowal published in the newspapers.

It was a month after this that the first intimation of the Sunday sailings appeared, in the form of a newspaper advertisement announcing that the "Emperor," a small steamer which had been plying for some years in the Gareloch trade, would leave Glasgow on Sunday, July 10th, at eight o'clock in the morning, for Kilmun, returning at a quarter past four in the afternoon, the return fares being 2/- in the steerage and 3/- in the cabin. Contrary to what one would expect, and certainly contrary to the practice of twenty years later, the notice bears that no intoxicating liquors will be sold on board.

Kilmun accepted the situation unprotestingly, but not all the dwellers by the Firth were such careless Gallios. In Rothesay, strict even among the orthodox, where even the pump-wells were padlocked on Saturday night and left in that condition till Monday morning, lest haply some thirsty wretch should profane the Sabbath by refreshing himself thereat, the prospect of a visit from the " Emperor " was not a matter that could be lightly disregarded. The " black-coats " of the town were aroused, and at a public meeting, called at the "spontaneously" expressed wish of the inhabitants, eloquence, six-parson-power, called forth a resolution affirming the obligation of the Sabbath and the determination of the meeting to oppose the threatened landing on that day by every means in their power. At the same time a committee was appointed to confer with the harbour trustees, who had themselves resolved to do their utmost to discountenance the innovation, but the occasion to act did not arise that season, the proprietors of the steamer ignoring Rothesay, although various routes, including Loch Goil and the Gareloch, were experimented with.

A curious incident took place on board the " Emperor " as she lay at the Bridge Wharf early in the morning of August 6th. One of the deck-hands who had been sleeping on board, happening to rise between four and five o'clock, found two feet of water in the engine-room and the vessel rapidly filling through an open sea-cock. Whether this was the work of some perfervid Sabbatarian, or simply a piece of carelessness on the part of the engine-room staff, it is impossible to say; the newspapers of the time assumed that it had been done maliciously, but similar incidents, due to carelessness, have been known to happen.

The " Emperor's " visits to the Holy Loch had been received with equanimity, but on the Gareloch a different reception was accorded them. Her first trip thither on the 1st of August appears to have passed off quietly, but that was merely the calm that precedes the storm. By the time of her next appearance on the 22nd of August the forces of orthodoxy had had time to make preparations for dealing with her. Sir James Colquhoun of Luss, proprietor of the old and new piers at Gare-lochhead, had publicly expressed his unqualified disapproval of the " Emperor's " visits. There is a fine old feudal flavour about the course pursued by the Laird of Luss. With a seignory

extending over a goodly portion of Dumbarton-
shire, where it might with truth have been said—

" The mossy knowes, the heathery howes, and ilka bonny
    park is his ;
The crofter's rent, the tinkler's tent, the ghillie's hard
    day's wark is his ;
The muircock's craw, the piper's blaw, and ilka collie's
    bark is his ;
The bearded goats, the tousy stots, and a' the braxy
    carcases,"

his zeal alike for the physical and moral welfare
of the inhabitants and for the conservation of his
own rights as proprietor led him to take drastic
measures to oppose the landing. Acting in his
capacity of Lord Lieutenant of the county, he
called out the local police, reinforcing them with
about twenty men in his own employment, with
orders to resist by force if necessary any attempt
which should be made to land at the pier.

As the steamer came alongside that Sunday
about twenty minutes past one, the passengers
found themselves confronted by this force, posted
behind a barricade of boxes, barrels and gangways
which had been erected for the purpose of increasing the difficulties of landing. The lessee of the
pier, powerless to oppose the will of the laird,
though doubtless sad at heart at the sacrifice of
pier-dues, explained to the captain of the steamer
that Sir James Colquhoun would not permit the
landing, and that, if the attempt were made, force
would be resorted to to prevent it, but the captain

absolutely refused to recognise the authority of Sir James and cast his mooring-lines ashore. They were promptly thrown back. The boat people, having procured a long pole, poked and pushed the defenders of the pier with it, but the latter succeeded in wresting it from them, and, using it as a lever, managed to force the steamer away from the pier. She was soon alongside again, and under a fusillade of coals, bottles, potatoes and turnips, the party on the pier were compelled to beat a retreat to the upper gate. A number of youths leapt ashore from the steamer, and after quickly demolishing the barricade and throwing the pieces into the water rushed to the upper gate, which they treated in similar fashion after a scuffle with the defenders. "While these disgraceful proceedings were going on," says the chronicler, "the banks of the loch were crowded by inhabitants who had gathered from considerable distances around, in anticipation that there would be a disturbance."

It was regarded as an aggravation of the case that this open defiance alike of Mosaic law and of the will of the Laird of Luss took place during divine service, and we are told that the excitement in the church was very great. Nor can it be wondered at that it was so among those who had not had the forethought to anticipate a disturbance, and one can sympathise with the zealots, penned within four walls and doomed to listen inactive to the sounds of war without, while the discourse dragged slowly through "firstly," "secondly," "thirdly," "lastly," "finally," "in conclusion," "in a word," and "one word more." Surely their cup was full when the inconsiderateness of a lady in fainting three times retarded the conclusion of the service and extinguished their last chance "to join the dreadful revelry."

Two persons, a deck-hand and a passenger of the "Emperor," were apprehended in connection with the disturbance and lodged in Dumbarton prison on a Sheriff's warrant, for examination, but nothing appears to have come of the proceedings.

On the following Sunday the "Emperor" found both old and new piers barricaded, but in spite of this succeeded in landing her passengers at the old pier. Fortunately, no personal violence took place, the objectors making no attempt

> "To prove their doctrine orthodox
> By apostolic blows and knocks,"

nor was there any rioting a week later, when, the excursionists having provided themselves with axes, the barricades offered no obstacle to their landing.

Baffled in his attempt to repel the invaders by force, the Laird of Luss had recourse to law, raising an action for interdict in the Court of Session, but the four judges before whom the case was tried concurred in refusing this. By the time this judgment was delivered in the middle of December the "Emperor" had been withdrawn for the season, and it was not until the following March that she revisited Garelochhead, when an orderly crowd was landed without molestation. Later in the season the steamer made her first Sunday trip to Rothesay, and the decorous behaviour of the excursionists afforded no loophole for adverse criticism, although it is said that a number of the objectors absented themselves from church for the purpose of keeping an eye on them.

Though the first round in the law-courts had ended in favour of the unregenerate, the Laird of Luss had no intention of letting the matter rest there. The case lasted for some years, and we have not followed it, but, as the Sunday steamers ceased calling at the private piers, it seems reasonable to suppose that he eventually made good his claim.

A BOX O' TRICKS

THE advent of the "King Edward" at the
beginning of the present century evoked great
public interest. In all the Clyde steamers, and in
all commercial steamships then existing, the method
of imparting a rotary motion to paddles or
screw did not differ in principle from that which
had been adopted in the "Charlotte Dundas" and
the "Comet." In this type of machinery the steam
from the boiler entering alternately at opposite
ends of a cylinder impels a piston backwards and
forwards. By the use of an eccentric the motion
of the piston itself is made to open and shut alternately the valves through which the steam is
admitted, so that the reciprocating motion is continued as long as the supply of steam is maintained.
A crank is employed to convert this reciprocating
motion into a rotary one, and thus paddles or screw
are made to revolve. But in the "King Edward"
cranks, eccentrics and slide-valves were all dispensed with. The steam, entering a drum, im-
pinged on a multitude of curved vanes or blades,
and imparted a rotary motion direct to the spindle
on which they were mounted. By this system a
saving in weight and bulk was effected, friction
and vibration were reduced and increased speed

secured, and the success of the "King Edward"
gave colour to the idea that the knell of the
reciprocating system had sounded, a view which
further experience has not borne out.

And yet the "King Edward" was not, after all,
the first Clyde steamer in which the reciprocating
principle had been discarded; she had been anticipated in this particular nearly half a century
before, in an experimental boat, known as the
rotatory steamer, which was placed on the river
by David Napier, but which, unlike most of the
experiments of that remarkable man, attained no
commercial success. No detailed description of the
machinery of this vessel is obtainable, but from
what we can gather it was in all probability a crude
form of turbine. We are told that it occupied very
little space, not more than the size of an ordinary
parlour table, and bore no resemblance to any
engine ever seen before. In outward appearance
it consisted principally of a complicated mass of
pipes, with two horizontal cylinders or steam-
chests, from which the paddle-shaft emanated.
Apart from the novel machinery, the rotatory
steamer was chock full of gadgets. Most of these
are set forth in a preliminary notice of the vessel,
which appears in the form of an advertisement in
the newspapers of 21st January, 1853. It runs:—
"The new patent rotatory steamer will commence
plying in February between Glasgow and Paisley.
Fares, Fore Cabin 3d., After Cabin 6d. The
advantages which these engines have over others

are that they are more compact, consume about a quarter less fuel and require no engineer. The steersman, by a peculiar valve, can move the vessel ahead or astern without communicating with anyone. The furnace-bars contain water, consequently the hot ashes, which are destructive to the common furnace-bar, in this case tend to the production of steam. There is also a simple application of the fan to assist combustion. These two parts of the patent might be applied with advantage to most of the steamers. These engines are not now matters of experiment. A steamer was fitted up with them in London above a year ago, and has been plying on the Severn with complete success, the engines being as perfect now as on the day they were made, and from the far-famed workmanship of the Clyde it is expected that the vessel will prove herself equal if not superior to the one made in London. Such steamers would be invaluable in crowded rivers like the Thames or Clyde, as running-down could scarcely ever happen, the steersman standing before the funnel, and there being no paddle-boxes to obstruct his view, he sees every object ahead and can stop or reverse the engines in an instant, without leaving the wheel or applying to any second party."

For a few weeks there was no further word of the steamer; she did not start sailing in February, and when she did start Dumbarton and not Paisley was her destination. From 23rd March she com·· menced her service, making two double journeys daily, downward at nine in the morning and half-past three in the afternoon, and upward at eleven in the forenoon and five in the evening. The fares were of the same modest amounts as those advertised to Paisley. A few additional particulars regarding the rotatory steamer are furnished by an engineer, who, noticing her as she lay at the steamboat quay getting ready for her maiden trip, and having an hour or two to spare, went on board and made the journey to Dumbarton and back. Her paddle-wheels, he says, were very small, each having only four floats, so that in lieu of paddle-boxes there was merely a bulge on each side under which the paddle-wheel worked, the bulwarks running right round the boat on one level. The pilot stood on a platform three or four feet above the deck and steered by means of a horizontal wheel. Close beside him were two long iron handles coming up from the engine-room, with which he started, stopped or reversed the engine as required. Considering the nature of the passenger's calling, something elucidating the principle of the engine might have been expected from him, and it is disappointing to find that he declines to enter into any minute description of it, and contents himself with describing its general appearance. No great speed was attained, the downward journey occupying an hour and forty minutes and the upward one an hour and a quarter, with a call at Renfrew in each instance, but from the point of view of economy the engine must have been

written down a success, a single waggon of coal
sufficing for two trips to Dumbarton and back.
The passenger is very non-committal in his expres-
sions regarding the steamer; the only feature of
which he directly expresses approval is the small
number of floats on the paddle, but he is not
satisfied with their shape and recommends the use
of wheels of greater diameter.

Within a few weeks the advertisements for the
rotatory steamer are discontinued and she never
reappears under that designation. We are inclined
to believe, however, that the following advertisement of 18th May, 1855, refers to the same
vessel:—

"Steamer 'Dumbarton,' Captain Campbell, com-
mences plying between Glasgow and Dumbarton
on Thursday, 24th May, leaving Glasgow at
12.30 and 5.30 afternoon, and Dumbarton at 8.30
morning and 2.30 afternoon. Although the proprietor of the 'Dumbarton' intends letting the
simplicity, economy and superiority of the engines
in every respect over others speak for itself, he
thinks it right to draw the attention of engineers
and steamboat proprietors to an article which is
out of sight and which may be comparatively
termed everlasting furnace-bars. They will not
only last for ever, but careless stokers cannot waste
any fuel, as any accumulation of fuel under the
bars tends to produce steam as well as that above.
They have been in use above three years, and
licences will be granted for these alone, and the

price of the licence will not be demanded until the party has six months' experience of their advantages over others. They are applicable to all kinds of furnaces, and if it were necessary can be replaced as easily as the common furnace-bars."

But we hear no more of the "Dumbarton." What a box of tricks she was! and what a lot of bright ideas were comprehended within that little craft! Rotary engine, forced draught, control of engine from the bridge, hollow furnace-bars— Captain Williamson informs us that she even had a surface-condenser and a water-tube boiler, working under the forced draught at a pressure of 120 lbs. to the square inch. He also tells us that the rotary engine, not proving a success, was removed and replaced by a pair of diagonals, the steamer being renamed "Gareloch" and placed in the Helensburgh trade until sold foreign. A steamer of that name, doubtless the same, plied between Greenock, Helensburgh and Gareloch-head throughout the years 1860 and 1861, and is not to be traced after the winter of 1861-2.

LOST BY STRANDING

STRANDINGS have been fairly numerous in the history of the Clyde fleet, involving in some instances serious damage to property, though happily life and limb have not suffered, yet the annals of a hundred and twelve years show only four instances of total loss through mishaps of this nature. These are all of ancient date, the oldest of them occurring nearly eighty and the latest nearly fifty years ago.

The first loss by stranding was that of the "Countess of Eglinton," a steamer built for the Largs and Millport station in 1844. Her career was very short, for in March, 1845, she broke from her moorings at Millport quay, and drifting on the Eilans became a total wreck.

The next of these happenings was due to sheer carelessness, a carelessness without parallel in the whole history of the service, for, however daring many of the old-time racing skippers were—and they certainly took risks now and then that were scarcely justifiable—lack of vigilance was never their failing; they were ever alert and skilful to extricate their vessels from tight corners. But crass stupidity and inattention were alone respon- sible for the throwing away of the "Eclipse." This smart little steamer, costing between £3000 and £4000, had been built in 1850 for the Dunoon and Kilmun service from the Broomielaw. The Castle Company, whose steamers were then enjoying a monopoly on that station, naturally regarded the new boat as an intruder, and took measures which, they hoped, would result in driving her off. Being a wealthy concern, they could afford to sacrifice money in order to accomplish their purpose; they accordingly advertised the fast steamer "Merlin" at the same hours as the "Eclipse," and reduced the fares at these hours to a few coppers. Each boat made two double journeys daily, so that the two were in constant competition, the rivalry reaching such a pitch that on more than one occasion the impatience of the skippers caused the engines to be started before the gangways were withdrawn, and passengers in the act of embarking were precipitated into the water. Matters reached such a pass that the Lord Provost of Glasgow, fearful lest some terrible disaster should occur, made representations to the Castle Company and induced them to alter the sailing hours of the "Merlin." The Company did not succeed in running the "Eclipse" off the route; she continued sailing throughout 1850, 1851, and 1852 with such success that in 1853 her owners were encouraged to build another steamer, the "Wellington," as a consort to her, and from May of that year the two boats maintained a daily service of two trips each way. A connection to

Arrochar was also established. The " Wellington "
and " Eclipse " continued plying as consorts during
the summer of 1854. On the 2nd of September
the " Eclipse," on the forenoon down-run from the
Broomielaw, was left in charge of a pilot, owing
to the illness of her skipper, Captain Barrie. About
midday, as the steamer approached Dunoon, the
pilot suddenly and quite unaccountably found himself steering straight for the Gantocks. He had
the engine reversed, but failed to get clear, and
the steamer was left hanging by the middle on a
ledge of rock, with the bow and stern over deep
water. The passengers with their belongings were
put safely ashore in small-boats; the pilot, terrified at
the result of his carelessness, fled and disappeared.
Measures were promptly taken for getting the
vessel off, but the day after the accident the strain
on the unsupported ends at low water proved
too great; she broke in two amidships, and all hope
of salving her was gone, though fortunately it was
found possible to recover the machinery. The
operations provided a great source of entertain-
ment for the Dunoon visitors; and the weather
being fine while they were in progress the scene
of the wreck was daily crowded with interested
spectators in small-boats. The engine salved from
the " Eclipse " was fitted into a new steamer called
the " Nelson," which plied for many years as a
consort to the " Wellington."

The stranding of the " Mars," seven months
later, occurred under altogether different circum-

stances. This steamer formed one of the celebrated M'Kellar fleet in the Largs and Millport trade, for which she had been built some ten years before. Although some newer steamers had appeared in the fleet, the "Mars" was still reckoned a good boat, and she had only resumed her station some ten days before the accident, after having undergone a complete overhaul. On the morning of 10th April, 1855, she left the Bridge Wharf at eight o'clock, in weather which is described as "very boisterous and stormy." However, she got along all right until approaching Largs, when her paddle-shaft unfortunately snapped, leaving her helpless. Sails were promptly hoisted in an endeavour to get her under control, but so high had the gale now risen that they were immediately blown away, and the vessel was driven ashore at the Gogo Burn. A man with a cart drove out into the water, with the view of rescuing some of the passengers, but found himself unable to get alongside; however, all on board got ashore without much difficulty. Half an hour afterwards the funnel fell overboard, and within two hours the "Mars" had gone to pieces so completely that scarcely a vestige of her was to be seen. The wrecked vessel was advertised to be put up by public auction at Largs quay on 24th April, but there is no record of a sale having been effected. It seems unlikely, as all that remained of the vessel must by that time have been scattered over several miles of coast.

"Mars" (*built 1845*)

The wreck of the " Mars " had followed rapidly on that of the " Eclipse," but nearly twenty-two years elapsed ere another of the Clyde river-steamers was lost by stranding while on her regular service, although there are one or two instances, such as that of the " Windsor Castle," where Clyde river-boats have been wrecked in the Firth after their connection with the river-trade had ceased. Messrs. Campbell & Gillies, who undertook the steamboat service in connection with the Wemyss Bay railway after the demise of the original Wemyss Bay Steamboat Company, had been content to maintain it economically with bought-in steamers till 1872, when they had a new boat built for them by Blackwood & Gordon. The " Lady Gertrude," as the new vessel was called, while by no means an outstanding boat, and of merely average speed, was certainly an improvement on anything the firm then possessed. Being intended for all-the-year-round work if required, she was flush-decked; her dimensions, 190 feet by 18 feet, approximated closely to those of several well-known steamers of the time, and, like most steamers of the 'seventies, she had an engine of the single diagonal type, with the boiler and funnel forward of the engine-house. From 1872 to 1876 the " Lady Gertrude " did the bulk of the work on the Wemyss Bay-Rothesay section. On a downward trip on Saturday, 13th January, 1877, as she approached Toward about noon, something went wrong with the reversing-gear, and as a gale was blowing down Firth the steamer, instead of stopping at the pier, went right on. Her stern striking the end of the pier caused the bow to swing inshore, and she went right on to the rocks. The steamer " Inveraray Castle " was passing at the time and attempted to tow the stranded vessel off by means of a hawser, but without success. Tugs were got from Greenock, and the steamer " Argyle," belonging to the same owners, lent her assistance and nearly shared the fate of her consort, for she actually went ashore but slipped off again. As the " Lady Gertrude " had gone ashore at high water, little hope of salving her was entertained from the first, and on Monday, 15th January, she broke her back, and the salvors had to rest content with recovering the engine, which was placed in the new steamer " Adela " and continued working on the Wemyss Bay route till 1890. Those who frequented Rothesay in the late 'seventies may recollect seeing the boiler of the " Lady Gertrude " on the shore at Toward Point, where it lay for several years.

Strange to say, neither the " Eclipse," the " Mars," nor the " Lady Gertrude " was insured; probably the payment of premiums was regarded as an expense which the lowness of the fares would not permit, and which the almost invariable good fortune of the Clyde boats rendered unnecessary.

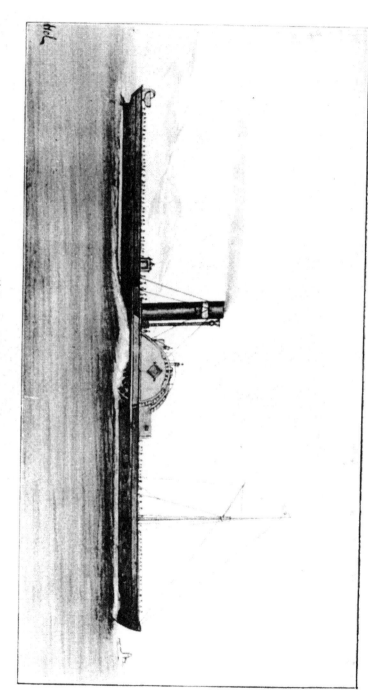

"Petrel" *(built 1845)*

" Glencoe " (*built 1846*)

Photo. by the Author

IN BOWLING BAY

When the chill winds and dark evenings of late autumn have driven the holiday-folks back to town the river-boats seek their winter quarters. A few there are that remain in commission, to carry on an attenuated service sufficient for the needs of the coast-dwellers during the winter months. Mostly small and economical boats are these, stripped of their summer finery and muffled up in winter-boards against the prospect of rough weather, but hardy, capable little vessels, not easily to be withheld from performing their journeys by any storm likely to be encountered within those limits beyond which, in the words of their Board of Trade certificates, " This ship is not to ply." Now and then, when winds are boisterous, the exposed position of some pier may deter them from risking a call, but under steam their stout steel hulls, propelled by such machinery as they turn out in the Clyde-side engine-shops, can bid the winds defiance. Even fog seldom prevents them from making their passages, though at such reduced speed as careful navigation dictates, for " schedule time " must yield when prudence bids, yet such are but infrequent happenings, and their services as a whole are maintained with a regularity that has few parallels.

F

But the " crack " boats of the summer fleet don no winter raiment. Not for them are the gales and fogs of that inclement season. Far too big for the meagre traffic, and far too expensive to keep in commission, they make their way to some snug harbour where they may rest secure until the gay season comes round again. The turbine boats and the steamers of the Caledonian and Glasgow and South-Western fleets have their dormitory at Greenock, and there they lie asleep all winter, dreaming perhaps of the glories of the past summer with its joyous rushes over seas radiant in the sunshine or silvered by the beams of the moon, when all was brightness and gaiety. Or perhaps, at other times, older recollections obtrude themselves, of encounter with submarine or of work among the mines in dirty weather (little sleep there was in those days), and make them twitch restlessly at the mooring-ropes, or maybe, on occasion, the spectres of those gallant lads in khaki may rise to haunt them, whom they bore across the Channel to France, but whom none ever brought back. For every one of these gay steamers donned the grey uniform at her country's call and played her part in the Great War gallantly and efficiently.

Even more of the boats seek the hospitality of Bowling Bay, and a winter visit to that sheltered haven is full of interest. There you will find them packed almost as closely as sardines in a tin, looking somewhat gaunt with all their portable deck-fittings removed and the familiar lifebuoys missing from

the rails, the bright colours faded and the gilt-
work tarnished by rain and fog; and grimy withal,
for metal and woodwork are encased in a coating
of sooty dust, to which every passing funnel on
river in front or railway behind adds its contribution. The "Columba," most famous of tourist-
steamers, whose tall red funnels stand out con-
spicuously against the dark background of the
Kilpatrick Hills, spends the greater part of her
lifetime at Bowling, her absences from the bay
never exceeding four months out of the twelve.
For most of the time she has for companion her
older sister, the "Iona," the wonderful old craft
whose excellence sixty years' plying has but little
impaired. The once-familiar black funnel with
white band that distinguished the Buchanan
steamers has been missing since the war, but the
vessels that bore it are there, now wearing the
white funnel with black top adopted on their
return to civilian life. Thither, too, come the
North British boats, the "Waverley," "Kenilworth," and "Talisman," not to mention the
"Marmion," whose war experiences would seem
to have ruined her constitution. Like many a
human war-victim she resumed her old occupation
on her return, but proved unfit for it, and an
operation performed on her has failed to restore
her to her former health. In an odd corner of the
bay there lay till lately a pathetic figure, the
"Marchioness of Lorne," once a smart-looking
member of the Caledonian fleet, but now unkempt

and neglected, bare of paint and battered, her upper-works looking like some decrepit hoarding after a gale. Towards the western end of the bay, close to Bowling pier and station, one may often see an old stager from the outer waters of the Western Highlands, with engine of the long-discarded steeple type and funnel perched well aft in the fashion that prevailed when the nineteenth century was still youthful. Her dreams (doubtless in Gaelic, for long service in the North must have made her as familiar with the language as she is with every sound and headland between the Mull of Kintyre and far-off Stornoway) will surely conjure up scenes of lofty mountains, with little thatch-roofed hamlets at their base, and broad-beamed ferry-boats rowed by brawny Highlandmen, as shaggy as the long-horned cattle on the shore, bringing alongside incredible loads of sheep, with, now and then, an odd passenger or two.

Bowling Bay, too, has been the last dwelling-place of many an old Clyde favourite, while the owners have been making up their minds that it was not worth while to spend money in over-hauling her. There the graceful old " Inveraray Castle," once an institution on the Inveraray station, and the " Athole," familiar as the four o'clock boat to Rothesay in the 'seventies and 'eighties, enjoyed a few seasons' respite from work ere the shipbreakers got them. The pretty little " Elaine," too, was broken up on the shores of the bay a quarter of a century ago, on the very spot

where that venerable relic, the "Industry," one
of the earliest of Clyde steamers, had been left
neglected until her stout old wooden hull fell to
pieces.

The association of the bay with the wintering
of steamers is of ancient date; probably it is coeval
with the steamboat herself, its sheltered situation
doubtless causing it to be early recognised as a
snug haven. Only on one occasion has it failed
to shield its occupants from the storm, and that
was when the great hurricane of 1856 struck the
Clyde valley. The disaster took place on the night
between the 6th and 7th of February, when many
of the river-steamers were laid up in the bay, and
the morning of the 7th brought to light an
appalling spectacle of destruction. The "Chancellor" (first of the name), a two-funnelled steamer
which plied to Arrochar, was lying on the breakwater with the water washing in and out of her.
The "Glow-Worm," a paddle-steamer, employed
between Ardrossan and Belfast, lay aground beside
her. The "Eagle" (also first of the name) had
got jammed between two other vessels, and so
badly buckled that the bell-mouths of her two
funnels (both abaft the paddles) were in contact.
The "Venus," of M'Kellar's Largs and Millport
fleet, had been stripped of her paddle-boxes and
sponsons; the Kilmun steamer "Wellington" had
sunk at her moorings; while two old steamers, the
"Merlin," the Largs and Millport boat, and the
"Invincible," which had been sailing to Rothesay

during the previous season, had been driven bow-on to the breakwater and were lying with their after-decks submerged. Strange to say, no one of the boats, with the possible exception of the " Merlin," which was not again advertised, was damaged beyond repair. The others all resumed their sailings when the summer season came round. Some of them survived for many years, the " Eagle " having an adventurous career as a blockade-runner in the American Civil War. Captured by the Federals, she was sold by them, and once more engaged in blockade-running, continuing to trade with the Confederate ports as long as the Confederates had a port for her to enter.

In February, 1855, just a year before the great hurricane, the steamers in Bowling Bay were frozen in, so that it was impossible to get them out, and the resumption of sailings to Loch Goil had to be postponed for a fortnight in consequence, but since these two exceptional years we cannot trace that frost or storm has ever caused any inconvenience to the occupants of Bowling Bay.

THE UPPER NAVIGATION

WHERE the Clyde river-steamer is mentioned, one naturally thinks only of the boats which have plied from the Broomielaw down-river towards the Firth, or on the Firth itself, and probably not many people are aware that there existed for a time a regular steamboat service *up-river* from Glasgow. Indeed, there seems reason to believe that such an enterprise has been started more than once, and that a small steamer plied for a time with passengers between Glasgow and Rutherglen about a hundred years ago, but no details of the vessel or particulars of her history have come down to us. A passenger steamboat service to Rutherglen was, however, set on foot and actually carried on in the 'fifties by Mr. T. B. Seath, whose name is so closely associated with the shipbuilding which for long formed an important industry in Rutherglen. Mr. Seath's first shipyard was at Meadowside, where he started business in 1854 and carried on for two years, during which time he built three steamers, two paddle and one screw. But the possibilities of the Royal Burgh as a shipbuilding centre fascinated him, and, although the wiseacres of the time shook their heads at what they deemed his folly, and prophesied disaster, he boldly transferred his business thither in 1856. The step justified itself by its success, and the Rutherglen business was carried on for nearly forty years, bringing good profit to its enterprising proprietor and helping to make the wee roon' red lums reek more briskly than ever before. During that period a very large number of vessels was launched, all comparatively small craft, for the narrowness and shallowness of the river there imposed limitations on the size; but the majority were of special designs for special employments which demanded superior workmanship, representing high value relatively to tonnage. Among them were many expensively fitted steam yachts, built to the order of various British aristocrats, as well as of some foreign potentates; fastidious customers, whose satisfaction with their vessels bears testimony to the work done at the Rutherglen shipyard. Of the commercial vessels constructed there, many were for services abroad, under conditions which called for exceptional strength, or shallow draught, or some other peculiarity of design. Among the biggest of the Seath productions were a number of river-boats, including " Vale of Clwyd," " Vale of Doon," " Bonnie Doons " (Nos. 1 and 2), " Windsor Castle," " Lucy Ashton " and " Isle of Arran," all of which might be reckoned successful boats. Of the two paddle-boats built at Meadowside, one was the " Nelson," employed for about fifteen years in the Kilmun trade; the other was the " Artizan," laid down by Mr. Seath for himself with a view to his projected

Cross-head of "Glencoe's" Steeple Engine

Photo: by the Author

Gilt Ornament on Companion of "Glencoe"

Photo by the Author.

service between Glasgow and Rutherglen. Her measurements were only 110 feet long by 12 feet wide, with a depth of about 7 feet, and she is said to have drawn only 27 inches of water. A contemporary picture shows her flush-decked, with no hurricane-deck or wing-houses, having two funnels placed forward and aft of the paddle-boxes, and no mast. Her engine was of non-condensing type, of 35 horse-power, and the speed about 12 miles an hour. The little steamer had good accommodation for passengers under deck, a saloon, 26 feet long, and a ladies' cabin being situated abaft the engines, while a fore-cabin, 22 feet long, was fitted up as a dining saloon and bar. Mr. Seath, who held both a pilot's licence and an engineer's certificate, acted in both of these capacities as well as that of skipper, having both the steering and the machinery under his control, the latter being started or stopped by means of a long lever which came up above the deck close to the wheel.

The enterprise was inaugurated on 29th May, 1856, the Queen's Birthday holiday, and the newspapers of the following day gave an account of the event in the following words:—" Upper Navigation of the River.—Yesterday afternoon not a little interest was manifested by a concourse of spectators who lined both banks of the river in the vicinity of Hutchesontown Bridge, to witness what may be considered a novelty, viz.—the starting of a steamer from the weir to Rutherglen quay. The boat, although not altogether suited for the station, was well patronised during the day, and on starting at one o'clock we observed several well-known city officials on board. Little surge was raised, and we presume that the aquatic sports, now so much indulged in on this part of the Clyde, will be little or nowise disturbed."

The Ancient and Royal Burgh fully appreciated the importance of the occasion, and her Provost and Magistrates, preceded by the Rutherglen Industrial Band and the Burgh officials in scarlet uniform, marched down to the quay, boarding the "Artizan" and sailing down the river to Glasgow. There the Provost mounted on the paddle-box and handed a speech to the Fiscal, which that dignitary read. The return to Rutherglen was followed by a dinner, at which, we may be sure, the success of the venture was well toasted.

Rowing, on the stretch above the weir, appears to have been a favourite pastime of the Glasgow youth of the period, and the advent of the "Artizan" evidently proved more of a nuisance than the author of the newspaper paragraph had anticipated, for, so early as 2nd June, a letter was published from a member of the Regatta Club, complaining bitterly of the way in which the running of the "Artizan" was interfering with the aquatic sports. A good deal of correspondence followed, showing that the navigation was rather ticklish, the maladroitness of some of the oarsmen and the obstinacy of others rendering it difficult to avoid collisions. The arrangement by which the skipper of the steamer had both wheel and engine under his immediate control proved an invaluable one under the conditions, for slowing, stopping, reversing or turning could be carried out without a moment's loss of time. A bell was rung to warn oarsmen who had got in the steamer's path, and if this warning went unheeded a bucket of water, kept handy on the fore-deck for the purpose, was thrown over the offender as a hint to make way. On the 5th of August the " Artizan " did collide with a small-boat and sink it, but the occupants got off with a ducking. Mr. Seath, however, had no desire to inconvenience or endanger the rowers unnecessarily, for he withdrew the steamer altogether on 29th and 30th August, when the annual regatta was in progress.

Up till the middle of September the " Artizan " made six trips daily in either direction, leaving Glasgow at 10.30 a.m., 12 noon, 2, 4, 6, and 8 p.m., and Rutherglen half an hour later. The single trip occupied a quarter of an hour or twenty minutes, and the fares were twopence in the steerage and threepence in the cabin. Return tickets at fourpence were issued, available in either end of the boat.

On 5th September Mr. Seath was entertained by a number of prominent Glasgow citizens to a complimentary dinner on board his vessel. The function lasted while the " Artizan " made two double journeys between Glasgow and Rutherglen,

and many eulogistic things were said of the steamer
and her enterprising proprietor. The Clyde Trustees
gave evidence of their goodwill to the undertaking
by erecting a small wharf or jetty at Hutchesontown Bridge for the convenience of passengers
landing and embarking.

About the middle of September the late evening
runs from Glasgow at eight and Rutherglen at
8.30 were discontinued, and six weeks later the
"Artizan" was withdrawn. During the time she
had been running some 36,000 passengers had
travelled by her. She did not reappear on the
Clyde, being sold to ply on the Lakes of Killarney,
but in September, 1857, another little steamer,
called the "Royal Burgh," took her place on the
Glasgow and Rutherglen station. She had been
launched with all due ceremony on 24th July, in
presence of the Provost, Magistrates, and Council
of Rutherglen. This boat, which was rather shorter
and broader than the "Artizan," measuring 102
feet by 14 feet, with engines of 45 horse-power,
plied during part of two seasons. On Saturday,
13th February, 1858, when laid up from the
Rutherglen station, she made a trip from the
Broomielaw to Lochgoilhead, returning on the
Monday following. The "Royal Burgh" went
to the Rhine in 1858, and was succeeded early in
the following season by the "Royal Reefer," a
rather bigger boat, measuring 133 feet by 13 feet,
with an engine of 50 horse-power, but ere long
the new boat was picked up for service on the

Neva, and as she was not replaced, the "Upper Navigation" enterprise came to an end, Mr. Seath, who had commanded all the boats, finding that the affairs of the shipyard required his presence there.

SPEED *VERSUS* COMFORT

In the 'fifties the Clyde steamer was rapidly developing into a speed machine pure and simple. Engine-power and perfection of model were the qualities that mattered, and the shipbuilding and engineering firms on the river had set themselves to outstrip one another in their productions. The oscillating type of machinery had been brought to great efficiency; never before had it been possible to develop such high power with engines so small and compact, and never before had engines been fitted into hulls whose lines were so well adapted to display their driving powers. Measuring as a rule some 200 feet in length, or perhaps a trifle less, with a breadth never much exceeding 18 feet, unsurpassed for fineness of entrance and cleanness of run, their hulls offered the minimum of resistance to the waves. Their sharp stems clove the water like knives, with no disturbance save a fine feather of spray, almost vaporous in its delicacy, rising in a graceful curve from the cutwater clear to the mainrail, till from a point some ten or a dozen feet abaft the stem a wave streamed aft at a narrow angle, while no unkindly curve of plate was allowed to deflect the broken water from the paddle-wheel in its rush to add itself to the sparkling wake. Fleet of foot and deep-chested were these vessels, for a couple of large haystack boilers gave them staying power. Never before had river formed course for such perfect thoroughbreds. Their owners, usually their builders, sportsmen all, saw to it that their favourites lacked no opportunity of displaying their prowess, providing them with skippers and engineers capable of getting the last ounce out of them, and not scrupulous about the observance of harbour regulations when racing was afoot. The skippers were constantly appearing at the police courts. "Failing to reduce speed when in harbour" was the usual charge; but the fines, ranging as a rule from one to three guineas, imposed by the magistrates, were cheerfully paid by the owner, all the more cheerfully if the commission of the offence had enabled his steamer to outstrip a rival or to clip a minute off the record between Glasgow and Dunoon.

Naturally, under such conditions, the accommodation of the passenger was a very secondary matter. Speed was everything, and nothing that would offer extra resistance or interfere with the vessel showing her best paces was tolerated. Consequently the deck-fittings were of the simplest, sufficient when the weather was fine, but affording no shelter in rain, while in the ill-ventilated cabins under deck the presence of a number of people soon rendered the atmosphere intolerably foul.

It seems to have occurred to a Mr. George Mills that there might be travellers who did not regard

speed as the one and only desideratum, to whom
a comfortable journey at a moderate pace would
appear more attractive than to be drenched or
stifled in a rush at breakneck pace for the sake of
passing all competitors or saving a handful of
minutes. He accordingly applied himself to the
designing of a vessel which, in his opinion, would
provide accommodation for all weathers, far more
comfortable than the Clyde service had ever known,
and which, while not exceptionally fast, should yet
possess a reasonable turn of speed. His design,
in which all the conventions were completely
departed from, was submitted to a number of
wealthy Glasgow gentlemen in 1854 and met with
considerable approval. Mr. Mills was advised,
however, to await the passing of the Limited Lia-
bility Bill, then before Parliament, and assured
that as soon as that measure became law he would
not lack support for his scheme of putting such a
vessel on the river. Consequently, it was not till
1856 that the Clyde Improved Steamboat Co.,
Ltd., was formed and the experimental steamer
" Alliance " laid down with Tod & M'Gregor.
The following description of her, published at the
time, shows how wide a departure she was from
the ordinary type of steamboat on the river : —

   " The vessel is so designed that it is equally
the same which end of her goes first, nay, so
constructed is a portion of her machinery that she
may be made to go laterally or sideways like a
crab, to back, to go ahead, or to turn round in

her own length like a pivot. Her shape is as follows: Let an ordinary Clyde steamer of say 140 feet long and 18 feet breadth of beam be taken, but with both ends alike, and be cut from end to end along the middle, each portion having one side built straight, so that it should form half a vessel. Let these two halves be placed at a suitable distance from each other, so as to allow a paddle to work in the trough formed between them. The two parts are bound together, first with horizontal strips or braces below water at the line of the keel, and again at the deck by means of beams and knees, the whole decked over and forming a broad, firm platform with nothing protruding above it except the wheel, for the machinery, boilers, etc., will be placed in the hulls below the deck. Large saloons, with sides principally of plate-glass, will be placed on this platform and the whole decked over as a promenade. Two small paddles, one at each end, worked by the donkey-engine, will be used for manœuvring at piers."

The vessel was duly built, and on Saturday, 3rd December, 1856, made a trial-trip down the river, but proved herself very slow. Mills had reckoned that she would steam fourteen miles an hour, but twelve was the utmost she achieved, and that only for a brief spurt, her average being far below even that modest figure. In manœuvring she was found to be all that could be desired.

On the 4th of April, 1857 (the Fast-Day holiday), the "Alliance" made her first trip with passengers to Garelochhead. She is said to have covered the distance in three and a quarter hours each way, no great performance, but considerably better than her trial-spin had given cause to expect, and as the day was cold and stormy, the comfort of her saloon was greatly appreciated. The "Alliance" made her next trip with passengers to Garelochhead on the Queen's Birthday holiday, Thursday, 21st May, and on the following Monday commenced plying regularly on that route. But whether it was owing to her unorthodox shape or her lack of speed, the public evinced no excessive desire to travel by her. Efforts were made to arouse some enthusiasm by means of newspaper articles extolling her attractions, the light and airy character of her saloon and the facilities she afforded for promenading in all sorts of weather. She was described as "not only the most comfortable, but the most luxuriously comfortable boat that was ever sailed on business or pleasure." As for speed, it was asked, "How many of the thousands who travel by river from Glasgow to Greenock ever do so for purely business purposes?" and the writer declares, "It is not so much speed that such travellers want as comfort." And, besides, he contends that the idea current that the "Alliance" is a slow boat is scarcely justified, as "she makes her run to Greenock in two hours, and there are very few boats doing it in less time." He claims for her that she is economical to work, and expresses his confidence in her success and his belief that patronage will be found not merely for one, but for half a dozen boats of her class.

But the " thousands who travel " did not display the same enthusiasm as the writer of the articles. The craze for speed was deeper-seated than Mr. Mills had supposed, and the " Alliance's " many attractions failed to reconcile the public to her lack of this essential. Though perhaps the aversion, springing from conservatism, which recoiled from her bizarre model might have disappeared in time, the indignity of being passed on the river by old craft long ago due at the shipbreaker's was an unpardonable failing. The claim for economical working, too, might have been accurate had the " Alliance " been allowed to crawl along at her own impossible pace, but to drive a vessel of such design even at twelve miles an hour involved a ruinous expenditure of fuel. So unprofitable did the boat prove that at the end of her second season the Clyde Improved Steamboat Co., Ltd., went into liquidation. Repeated attempts to sell the steamer proved abortive. She was offered for sale by auction no less than six times during the months of January, February and March, 1859, the upset price, originally fixed at £4500, coming down gradually to £1500, but even then the offer found no takers. The liquidator then advertised her for charter by pleasure parties and others, and eventually got her let for the Sunday trade, but even in that last refuge of the destitute and in-

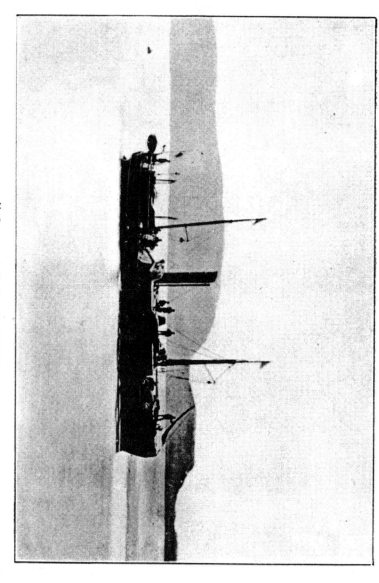

Photo. by Messrs. McIsaac & Riddle, Oban

"Cygnet" (*built 1848*)

competent she was not a success, and at the end of the season was completely withdrawn from the service. She did not appear in the advertisements of 1860, but in July, 1861, plied for a short time on the Caledonian Canal, and those who are familiar with the present scale of fares on that route will learn with surprise that half a crown sufficed to carry the passenger from Inverness to Banavie in the second cabin of the " Alliance," while the payment of an additional half-crown entitled him to all the comforts of the first saloon.

Her next appearance was on the Mersey, but with no better fortune, until, after being laid up and vainly offered for sale, she was eventually picked up for blockade-running and sailed for Nassau in August, 1863. It is notorious that a slow boat was often more successful than a swift one in that occupation, and the experience of the " Alliance " seemed to bear this out, as she made several trips before being captured at Savannah in April, 1864, and doubtless proved a profitable ship to the speculator who bought her.

The next word we hear of the " Alliance " is from a New Zealand paper, the " West Coast Times," in the autumn of 1865. It seems that, after falling into the hands of the Federals, the steamer was taken to New York and there put up for sale by auction and knocked down to a Boston firm, who made considerable alterations on her and sent her out to Melbourne, Victoria, where she traded for a short time. Then a discovery of gold was made on the west coast of New Zealand, causing the usual rush to the district, and the "Alliance" was sent thither to secure a share of the traffic. As the "Three-funnelled, covered-decked paddle-steamer 'New Zealand'" she was set to ply between Dunedin and the gold district. She made one very successful double journey, but on her second trip went ashore at the entrance to the harbour, broke her back and went to pieces. Her passengers were successful in escaping, but a large portion of her valuable cargo was lost. Thus ended the eventful, if somewhat inglorious, career of this interesting but unsuccessful steamboat. She had been but nine years afloat, first as a Clyde river-boat, partly as a Sunday-breaker, next on the Caledonian Canal, then on the Mersey, with a spell laid up in dock, following which came a turn of blockade-running, capture and conveyance to New York, sale and despatch to Melbourne, and after some service there transference to the New Zealand coasting trade, where her adventures terminated in the manner described. So that this first Clyde saloon steamer had no lack of variety in the experiences of her short lifetime. The pity is that for the purpose for which she was designed the "Alliance" was a failure, and that the ingenuity and courage of Mr. Mills brought him nothing but disappointment.

THE EVENTFUL VOYAGE OF THE "PETREL"

One of the finest of the river-steamers built for the Clyde service during the 'forties was the "Petrel," launched by Barr & M'Nab at Paisley in 1845. Her handsomely-modelled though rather crank hull measured 165 feet in length by 17 feet 4 inches in breadth and 9 feet in depth, dimensions exceeding those of most of the river-boats then plying, while her steeple-engine of 90 horse-power placed her among the fastest of her time. For the first ten years of her career she plied principally on the Rothesay station. In each of these years new steamers had been placed on the river, embodying improvements due to the development of the shipbuilding and engineering crafts, so the owners of the "Petrel," finding her perhaps just slightly behind the times, deposed her in favour of a more up-to-date vessel and put her in the market. She was accordingly offered for sale by auction in November, 1855, but failed to find a bidder willing to pay the reserve price of £2400 placed on her. In the beginning of December a half-share in the "Petrel" was put up at £1000, and at this price a purchaser was probably found, as two months afterwards the steamer was sailing to Lochgoilhead. From the autumn of 1857 till the following midsummer she lay in Bowling harbour, being repeatedly offered for sale without result, while the upset price underwent a gradual reduction, first to £1500, then to £1300, and ultimately to £1000. At the last-named figure she eventually changed hands. Up to that time there was only one steamer, the " Emperor," plying on the river on Sundays, and the new owner of the " Petrel," convinced that sufficient support could be found for a second boat, decided to run her on that day. The steamer was certainly in need of some repairs, and work was begun on these, but the coasting season was then at its height, and every day's delay meant loss of valuable trade, so it was deemed advisable to place her on the station without waiting for their completion.

The first Sunday trip was accordingly advertised for 11th July, at 10 a.m., the destination being the Kyles of Bute. In conveying a pleasure-party down the river on the previous day the " Petrel " had come to a standstill off Port-Glasgow, and it was not until a number of tradesmen had been taken on board and set to the repairing of some defects that she could be got to proceed. Despite this inauspicious start it was decided that she should sail on Sunday as advertised. How far she was from perfect is evidenced by the fact that the donkey-engine, used for filling the boiler, was not in working order, so that some of the crew had to be detailed to maintain the necessary supply by means of a hand-pump.

A crowd of passengers boarded the "Petrel" at the harbour that Sunday morning, and at ten o'clock she cast off her mooring-ropes and set forth on a voyage that was to prove full of incident. She had got no farther than Govan when the passengers on the hurricane-deck found themselves subjected to a deluge of hot water from the steam-pipe. No one was seriously hurt, but, in the language of a contemporary scribe who never uses a short word where a long one will serve, "The apparel of several passengers was irretrievably ruined by the unexpected vapouring." This appears to have been the only mishap on the outward journey; the really exciting incidents were reserved for the homeward run after Greenock had been passed. It is highly probable that these were to a great extent due to causes quite unconnected with the condition of the steamer. It seems that, although the advertisement had set forth that no spirituous liquors would be sold on board, this regulation had been merely a concession to appearances and was completely ignored in practice, whisky being supplied in any quantity to anyone willing to pay for it. If there was no lack of liquor there was no lack of customers for it, so much so that the vessel's stock of glasses and tumblers was found quite inadequate. As tea was not in demand, the dishes usually devoted to that beverage were appropriated to supply the shortage of glassware, and the more potent fluid was dispensed in tea-cups and egg-cups, and even in sugar-basins and slop-bowls.

What wonder if the vessel's course was some-what erratic as she steamed up the river, taking the full width of the channel, so that she almost stumbled on the bank at Port-Glasgow, and was only saved by stopping and backing, while fuddled women passengers fainted and were escorted below by their no less fuddled cavaliers, to weep maudlin tears into the liquor-charged crockery over their perilous plight.

Meantime those in charge of the steamer had been so absorbed in getting her clear of the danger of the bank that they had failed to notice a new peril in the form of a number of empty mud-punts lying moored right in her path. Their presence was only detected when the steamer was within twenty yards of them, but stopping and backing were again resorted to with success. But the river that day was strewn with dangers for the poor "Petrel," for no sooner was she clear of the punts than a fresh obstacle presented itself, a coal-laden smack lying directly ahead and but a short distance off. For once the "Petrel" kept a straight course, striking the smack fair and true on the quarter, but thanks to the slanting form of the steamer's bow—a fashion favoured in those days—the damage stopped a few inches above the water-line, and the crew of the smack, by throwing a portion of the cargo overboard and shifting the position of another portion, were able to keep her afloat. While they were thus engaged the steamer stag-gered past, heading for Bowling, where a dozen

or so of passengers awaited her at the lower wharf.
When Bowling was reached the position of the
wharf does not appear to have been very clearly
observed on board the steamer, for she missed it
altogether. Once more the "Petrel" was stopped
and backed, but this time she resented the process,
and snapping her rudder-chains lay across the river
quite unmanageable. The futility of attempting to
get alongside Bowling wharf was recognised, and
the attempt abandoned, and the engine was again
put in motion. By this time the bow had swung
round and was pointing straight for the upper
wharf. With the rudder out of control there was
no means of steering the steamer, and the pilot,
realising this, bawled frantically to the captain to
stop, but that officer, either not having learnt of
the breaking of the rudder-chains or having perhaps forgotten the circumstance, paid no attention.
"Then," says the chronicler, "the pilot, as a last
resource, inserted the tiller and turned the helm
in time to pass the wharf by about a foot." One
cannot help thinking that the insertion of the tiller
when the chains broke would have been the first
and not the last resource of a pilot with his wits
about him.

From this point surely some good fairy must
have taken matters in hand and guided the poor
befuddled "Petrel" up the river, for she reached
Glasgow without further mishap, and save for some
scraping of paint at the bows and perhaps a dented
plate or two where she had come in contact with

the smack, none the worse for her adventures. A few days later the skipper appeared at the police court and was fined £1 for the affair of the smack.

Towards the end of July it was reported in the newspapers that a half-share in the " Petrel " had been purchased by the master of one of the river-steamers and that she would thenceforth cease to sail on Sundays, but this proved inaccurate, as the steamer remained in the Sunday trade.

Anyone who loves a good boat must deplore that the " Petrel " fell into such evil hands. That she was a good boat is certain, for she lasted forty years, although for a long period she experienced nothing but abuse and neglect.

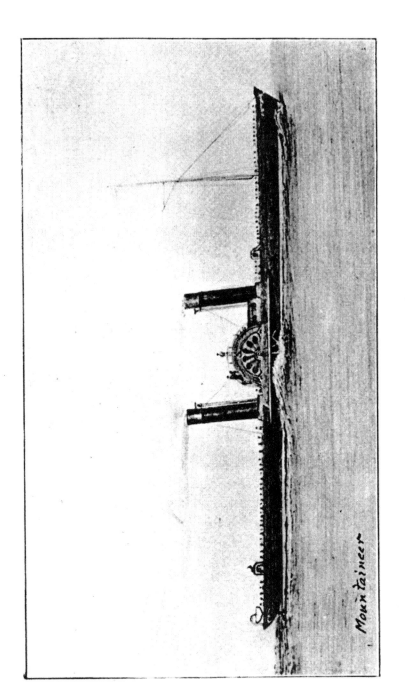

"Mountaineer" (*built 1852*)

Photo from a Drawing in Mr. Hubbard's collection

RECORD-MAKERS OF THE ROTHESAY ROUTE

A NOTABLE feature in the history of the Clyde steamers is the rapid improvement in speed that took place between sixty and seventy years ago. When, in 1852, the " Mountaineer " on her trials ran the lights at the rate of fifteen knots she was hailed as the swiftest steamer afloat, but within a very few years there were steamers plying on the Firth which could have left her miles behind on that short run. Her successor, the first " Iona," launched in 1855, proved herself a seventeen-knot boat, and the " blue riband " was promptly claimed for her, but there were at least half a dozen steamers at the time or within a year or two whose performances show that they would have been well entitled to challenge her claim to the distinction. Which was really the fastest is a question which formed the subject of many an acrimonious dispute at the time, and which is still an open one, so that it would be unprofitable now to hazard an opinion; certainly the skipper of each was confident in the superiority of his own boat and prepared to demonstrate it against all comers.

The Broomielaw-Rothesay route was the favourite racecourse; the boats were competing there not only against one another but against the

Glasgow and Greenock Railway, and the runs which they made stand to this day as the fastest on record.

In the early spring of 1854 two of the firms running steamers to Rothesay included in their lists of vessels " New steamer, now building." The names afterwards conferred on these two steamers were " Ruby " and " Rothesay Castle," and no two names are more celebrated in the annals of the Clyde. There have been five " Rothesay Castles," and the steamer of 1854, known as " Caird's Rothesay Castle," was the third of these, but of the five this one and her immediate successor were the only ones possessing exceptional speed. The " Ruby " was the first and least remarkable of three steamers of the name, all built by Henderson of Renfrew, but a boat of more than average speed all the same, a fact which her skipper, Captain Richard Price, lost no opportunity of demonstrating. Price had a perfect mania for racing, and was constantly being fined for ignoring the river regulations. That he was an obliging man the following story would seem to prove. Once when the " Ruby " was on her afternoon run direct from the Broomielaw to Gourock, a passenger bound for Dumbarton, who had come on board under the impression that the steamer called there, approached the skipper with the request to be landed at Dumbarton if possible. Price refused to call, but, pointing to the Dumbarton boat, which the " Ruby " was rapidly overhauling, offered to pass her so close that the passenger might step from one paddle-box to the other, although, as he explained, the exploit would probably involve breaking something. The passenger, however, being less of a sport than the captain, elected to go on to Gourock and return home to Dumbarton by another boat.

But, notwithstanding her skipper's energetic driving, no record passages of the first "Ruby" are to be traced.

Caird's "Rothesay Castle" was evidently a faster boat. After a single season on the Rothesay route she was placed in the Ardrishaig mail service, her hours being identical with those of the "Columba" to-day and her route the same except for a call at Strone. In 1856 she was back on the Rothesay station, taking the favourite four o'clock run from the Broomielaw. On the 1st of October in that year she reached Dunoon pier at 5.57, and, taking matters easily from that point, proceeded to Innellan and Rothesay, arriving there at 6.41.

The engines of the "Rothesay Castle" were of diagonal, and those of the "Ruby" of oscillating, type. Those of the "Pearl," built by Henderson as a consort to the "Ruby" in 1858, were diagonal, but of peculiar construction, with four cylinders operating a single crank, an arrangement that has never been repeated on the Clyde. Probably it was not found to be an advantage in developing speed, for she was never placed on the morning and afternoon express runs, her usual sailing hour being 10 o'clock from the Broomielaw and 2.30 from

Rothesay. The people who travel at that time of day are seldom in any particular hurry.

In 1859 Caird produced a consort for the "Rothesay Castle," and a very noteworthy boat she was. Determined that she should be a flier, and fully alive to the advantage of lightness and shallow draught, her builders took the bold course of constructing her of steel, a material of which no Clyde steamer had yet been built. So confident were they of its qualities that plates of unexampled thinness were used, those at the keel being only five-sixteenths and those at the deck-line one-eighth of an inch in thickness. As a consequence she drew when launched only 21 inches of water, and even with a powerful double diagonal engine on board her draught was only 3 feet. It was originally intended that this steamer should be called "Dunoon Castle," but some time before the launch, which took place on 5th May, the name had been altered to "Windsor Castle." The "Ruby," "Rothesay Castle," and "Pearl" were two-funnelled, but the new boat had a single funnel forward of the engine-house. She was fitted with a superheating process for steam, and had an expansion valve by which the speed could be increased for a short spurt when desirable. This contrivance was found very useful when the steamer was racing a rival for a pier, where a few minutes' stoppage gave her opportunity to recover breath. Captain Malcolm Campbell of the "Rothesay Castle" took command of the

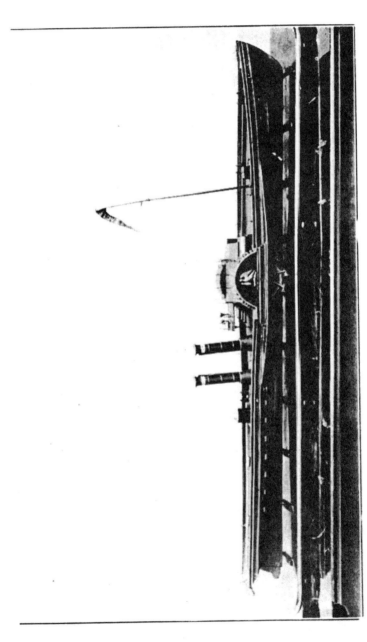

Model of "Eagle (I)" (*built 1852*)

In Kelvingrove Art Galleries

Photo. by Messrs. T. & R. Annan & Sons

" Windsor Castle," his pilot, Charlie Brown, being promoted to the paddle-box of the older boat. Under these two skippers the boats were hard driven. Each made three single journeys daily between Glasgow and Rothesay, the steamer that lay at the Broomielaw one night spending the following night at Rothesay and *vice versa*. An arrangement had been come to with the owners of " Ruby " and " Pearl " so that the sailings of these boats did not clash with those of the "Castles." On Friday, 10th June, 1859, the " Windsor Castle," leaving Rothesay at 7 a.m., reached the Broomielaw at 9.35, a feat which was equalled by the " Rothesay Castle " the next morning.

What became of the first " Ruby," or even the exact date of her withdrawal from the service, we have not been able to trace; the name never disappears from the advertisements, for a second " Ruby," built in 1860, took her place on the station in June of that year. She was a bigger boat than her predecessor, and had powerful diagonal oscillating engines. Captain Price was put in command, and found her a speed instrument after his own heart, responsive to every touch of the master. We have not traced any of her Broomielaw-Rothesay records, but on a Saturday evening trip at the end of June she sailed round Bute in 2 hours 15 minutes, which was stated to be by far the shortest time in which the journey had ever been made. But the " Ruby " was capable of far greater

things, for on 4th August she made the same trip
in 2 hours 0 minutes 30 seconds. A few days later
she ran the lights with a party of 150 on board,
and was clocked to cover the distance in 46 minutes
30 seconds, a rate of about $17\frac{1}{2}$ knots. One would
think that such a pace required no apology, but
attention is called to the fact that she was retarded
by a head-wind and also to some extent by having
so large a party on board. It is characteristic of
the reports of speed trials about this period that
some adverse condition has always been present to
prevent the vessel displaying her full powers.

During June, July, and August, 1860, these
four steamers maintained a service of five sailings daily to Rothesay and back, but on 3rd
September an announcement appeared in the newspapers that the two " Castles " would cease plying
after the 4th. According to a paragraph in the
same issue, they had been sold for service on an
Indian river, and were about to be fitted out for
the voyage thither.

Their machinery was removed and shipped out
separately. The hulls, shorn of the paddle-boxes
and wings, were strengthened with metal stringers
in the vacant engine-rooms, and with elm planking
screwed on internally round the window-strakes
and at other vulnerable places. Rigged as three-
masted schooners, they were despatched under sail,
and trouble began. The " Rothesay Castle " put
into Waterford through stress of weather, made
repeated attempts to get away, and as often returned

to some Irish port. After nine months of this, she reached Greenock in tow at the end of June, 1861, and the attempt to sail her out having been abandoned as futile, she was taken to pieces and sent out by sailing-ship.

The tribulations of the " Windsor Castle " were more quickly over. On the morning of 27th September she sailed from Lamlash Bay in lovely weather and with a north-easterly breeze so gentle that her progress was only from two to two and a half miles an hour. By eleven o'clock at night she was well down the Kintyre coast, and after setting a course to take her through the Sound of Sanda her skipper, Captain Walker, who had been on deck since four o'clock in the morning, retired below, leaving the mate in charge. But the influence of the currents on her long hull with its trifling draught was much greater than had been reckoned; she worked rapidly shorewards, and in spite of all efforts to keep her off went gently ashore, broadside on, at half-past one in the morning. Rockets were fired, and the 'Derry steamer " Falcon " coming along, the crew of the " Windsor Castle " were given the chance to leave her, but refused, being convinced that they were in no great personal danger. Though the weather was perfect, the swell of the Sound of Sanda proved too much for the flimsy steel plates; they speedily buckled and snapped on the rocks, the vessel filled, and her destruction was complete, the crew making their way ashore in safety.

The "Ruby" and "Pearl" continued plying throughout September; at the end of that month the "Ruby" was withdrawn, and that finished her service on the Clyde, for on 6th November she was sold to the same firm who had bought the two "Castles." Fitted out in similar fashion, she sailed on 19th November, but although three surveyors pronounced her perfectly seaworthy, her crew were less satisfied, and several of them deserted. She left Lamlash short-handed on 23rd November, under a Captain Frost, who announced his intention of calling at Queenstown, to make up her complement. But she never reached Queenstown. The story of her loss is just that of the "Windsor Castle" over again, except that it happened on the County Down coast, and that it was under the rays of Copeland Light instead of Sanda that her crew made their way ashore.

Perhaps it was fortunate that these two vessels came to grief where they did. Had they got to sea it is not improbable that the "Lutine" Bell would have sung their requiem.

New hulls were built and sent out to India, to receive the engines of the "Ruby" and "Windsor Castle." It is interesting to learn from a Calcutta newspaper of 21st March, 1862, that the "Soane," into which those of the "Ruby" were fitted, fully maintained the prestige of her illustrious predecessor, running an officially-measured nautical mile on the Hooghly in 3 minutes 14 seconds, and a distance of seventeen statute miles in 45 minutes.

The former performance is credible, the rate being just over $18\frac{1}{2}$ knots, to which, no doubt, current and tide contributed, but the other, averaging fully a knot more over a longer distance, is at least open to doubt. The roundness of the figures does not inspire confidence. The times given for such distance tests at that period were always expressed in minutes and half-minutes, with a fine disregard of seconds. In the present instance, too, there is no suggestion that a seventeen-mile course was accurately measured and marked off by posts, and we can well believe that a timekeeper, enthusiastic on the subject of the vessel's powers, would see to it that she suffered no injustice in the determination of the starting and finishing points.

Le Roi est mort; vive le Roi! Early in the summer of 1861 a new " Ruby " and a new " Rothesay Castle " were on the Rothesay station and the piling-up of new speed records was going on as merrily as ever.

THE PALMY DAYS OF RACING

When the three crack Rothesay steamers, "Rothesay Castle," "Windsor Castle" and "Ruby," were sold off the river late in the season of 1860, preparations were made for replacing them. Messrs. James Henderson & Son laid down a new "Ruby" rather bigger than their short-lived crack, the engines being of the same diagonal oscillating type which had proved so successful in her case, but of slightly increased power. This particular design of engine had been patented by Mr. J. M'Clintock Henderson, and no other boats had yet been fitted with it. Messrs. Caird did not re-enter the field, but a new "Rothesay Castle" was laid down by Messrs. William Simons & Co., of Renfrew. Her engines were oscillators of the usual type. Messrs. Napier, too, owners of the handy little "Vulcan," which they had built seven years before, determined to have a boat which should be in the first flight, and with this object set about building the "Neptune." She was diagonal-engined, with very small paddle-boxes, and a peculiarity of her appearance was that there were no wing-houses on the sponsons. Public attention appears to have been more attracted to the new "Ruby" than to either of the other two.

At the middle of March a newspaper paragraph appeared, mentioning that her construction was making rapid progress. Her predecessor of the name had been an exceptionally fast boat, and it seemed not unreasonable to expect that the builders, after a season's experience of her, would be able to produce something faster still. The "Rothesay Castle," building in the adjacent yard, was not mentioned in print until the time of her launch, in the second week of May, and then only in a few lines, giving her dimensions, and stating that she had been launched with her machinery on board, and was intended to be employed in the Rothesay trade. Probably the fact that Messrs. Simons had not built any steamers for the river trade before prevented any extravagant expectations regarding her. Robert Napier's great reputation as a shipbuilder and engineer was sufficient guarantee that the "Neptune" would be a good boat, but his triumphs had been more in channel and ocean-steamers than in river-craft, and it is evident that public confidence centred mainly in the "Ruby." While the three boats were fitting out, a letter signed "Visitor" was published in "The Glasgow Herald," in which the writer offered to bet £100, level, that Henderson's boat would beat both Napier's and Simons's boats either in "running the lights" or in a race from the Broomielaw to Rothesay, either Professor Rankin or the Surveyor of the Board of Trade to act as referee. It is not at all likely that the challenge

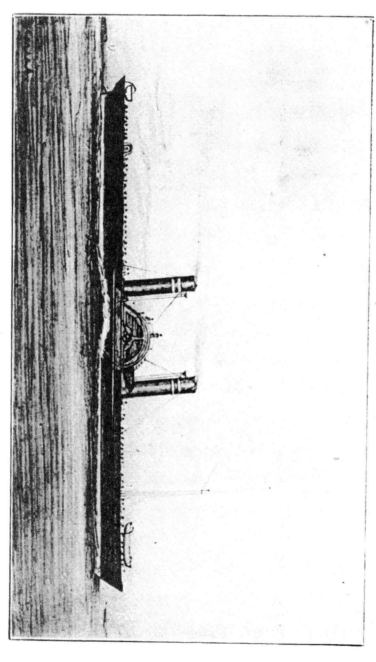

"Venus" (*built 1852*)

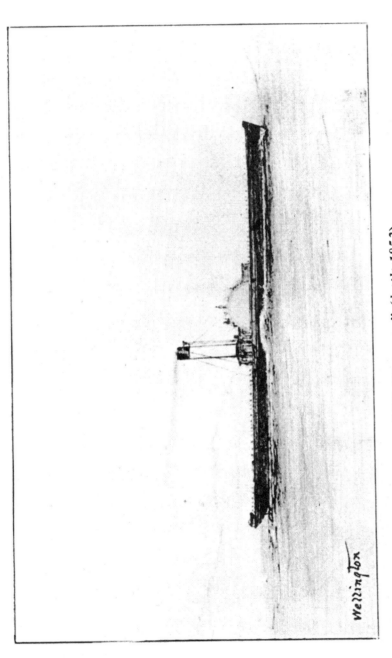

"Wellington" (*built 1853*)

Photo. from a Drawing in Mr. Hubbard's collection

was accepted, but the incident is worthy of notice as indicative of the interest which the rivalry had created.

On the 24th of May the " Ruby " went down the river for a preliminary spin through the Kyles of Bute to Ardlamont, but there is no hint of her speed having been timed over any measured course. Several steamers were encountered and raced with, among them being the " Neptune," which had not yet been placed on her station, and an easy victory was claimed for the " Ruby " in her case as in all the others. Perhaps the ease with which it was accomplished was less apparent on board the " Neptune"; judging by the speed which this vessel is known to have attained, there cannot have been much between the two boats. Their sailing hours, however, gave them no opportunity of trying conclusions on service.

It was otherwise with the " Ruby " and " Rothesay Castle." Both were deliberately scheduled to start at the same hours, viz.—7 a.m. from Rothesay and 4 p.m. from the Broomielaw, with no intermediate calls between Glasgow and Gourock. Their first encounter took place on the afternoon of Saturday, 25th May. The newspaper report, following the invariable custom in such cases, denies that there was any attempt at racing, although " considerable interest was manifested both at the Broomielaw and along the coast by crowds of persons who were in expectation of witnessing a race." It is admitted, all the same, that the boats "steamed in a most admirable manner, while the 'Ruby' proved herself to be the swifter vessel," reaching Gourock in an hour and 35 minutes, with the "Rothesay Castle" less than a minute behind. Rothesay, where their respective merits formed the universal topic of conversation, was reached by the "Ruby" at 6.44, three minutes ahead of the Simons boat. These were good runs, although the times were not by any means records; perhaps some slight adverse weather condition may have been present or the new machinery may not just have reached perfect working order; at any rate, it was soon to appear that the boats were capable of much faster work.

It had been arranged that the steamers were to change berths at the Broomielaw on alternate days, and on Monday, 27th May, the advantage of lower berth fell to the "Rothesay Castle." Right well she availed herself of it, for, having the lead, she kept it, travelling as never steamer had travelled on the river before. At twenty minutes past five the spectators on the Custom House Quay at Greenock saw her race past, with the "Ruby" in close attendance. Keeping up the pace, the "Rothesay Castle" finished at Rothesay quay two and a half minutes ahead of her rival, having covered the distance in 2 hours 28 minutes, a performance never equalled before or since. The feat was suitably recognised, the awards being made the following Monday by Bailie Raeburn at the River-Bailie Court, where Captain Brown of the "Rothesay Castle" was

fined a guinea for reckless navigation, and Captain
Price of the "Ruby," in view of the reputation
he had acquired for similar exploits, double the
amount. A further fine of half a guinea was
imposed on Captain Price at the same time for
passing Erskine Ferry at the gallop on 31st May,
but nothing is said as to the time then made by
the "Ruby." As that steamer had been withdrawn to undergo some slight alteration on 29th
and 30th May, it is evident that Price had not
lost many opportunities of getting into trouble.
On these two days the "Pearl" had opposed the
"Rothesay Castle" on the four o'clock express
run, but naturally had no chance, although a run
of 2 hours 46 minutes proves that her speed was
far above the average.

The following week the racing ceased, and the
"Ruby" and "Rothesay Castle" were running
as consorts, each making three single journeys in
the day, so that they took the four o'clock express
run alternately. They continued to make good
times, the "Ruby" accomplishing the morning
up-run on 19th June in 2 hours 31 minutes, and
landing her passengers before the 8.45 train from
Greenock, but the time made by the "Rothesay
Castle" on 27th May was never beaten, and stands
as the record to this day.

A gentleman long since dead used to give a vivid
description of that day's famous contest. He had
strolled down to the Broomielaw simply for the
purpose of seeing the two new steamers, and,

unable to resist the fascination of a race, determined to sail down the river to Gourock and return
from Greenock by rail. He accordingly went on
board the " Rothesay Castle." The " Ruby," he
said, showed herself to be slightly the faster boat
in the upper part of the river, gradually closing up
the hundred yards or so of daylight that had
separated them at the start, until, by the time
Bowling was reached, a passenger standing at the
stern of the " Rothesay Castle " could have touched
her bows with a walking-stick. A perspiring fireman came up from below to cool himself on deck
and see how the race was progressing, and as he
stood wiping the sweat and coal-grime from his
forehead with an oily rag, a passenger had the
temerity to ask him " Are you not going to slow? "
The fireman demanded in picturesque language
what ground could be found for such a proceeding,
and on the passenger explaining that " That boat'll
be in through you if you don't," voiced his scep-
ticism in very forcible terms. He prophesied that
" As sune's we get into deeper water, ablow Dumbarton, we'll leave her staunin'." His forecast of
events was so far verified that from the point named
the " Rothesay Castle " began gradually to increase
her distance, and had gained appreciably by the
time Greenock was passed, but as she approached
Gourock the struggle had become so keen that any
failure to take the single berth at the pier cleanly
would have allowed the " Ruby " to cut inside.
One of the passengers, an old Naval Reserve man,

who had become greatly excited, shouted a warning to the captain, and, springing up beside the pilot, seized the wheel and lent his assistance in bringing the steamer alongside with a bump that sent the passengers staggering and a crash that told of splintered wood at the paddle-box. The "Ruby" had come so close up on the chance of cutting out her rival that she was forced to back out to recover steerage-way ere she could come alongside, and by the time her gangways were withdrawn and her mooring-ropes let go the "Rothesay Castle" was well on her way towards Kirn.

On the 9th of July the "Ruby" accomplished a remarkable feat in steaming round Bute in 1 hour 56 minutes 30 seconds, 4 minutes and 10 seconds faster than the record established by the second "Ruby" in the previous summer.

But Price was determined to have a race with the "Neptune," and on the 27th of July he accomplished his desire. He was on the morning run, leaving the Broomielaw at 6.45. On this trip the steamer was scheduled to call at Greenock and Gourock and the usual ports from there to Rothesay. The "Neptune" made an early run up from Rothesay to Greenock in connection with the railway, and then returned empty to Rothesay direct for a second trip. On this occasion she was just about to leave Greenock as the "Ruby" arrived there, and you may be sure that Price did not lose much time before starting in pursuit. Captain Sandy M'Lean (afterwards so well known and highly respected as the owner of " Marquis of Bute " and " Athole "), who was in command of the " Neptune," was very averse to racing. He accordingly slowed up and stopped his steamer off the Albert Harbour to allow the " Ruby " to pass. But that did not accord with Price's ideas. He wanted a race and he meant to have it, so no sooner had he passed the " Neptune " than he slowed up and stopped his vessel also. Could such a challenge be ignored? Not likely! The two steamers were at it tooth and nail in a twinkling. Past Gourock, where Price should have called, they raced at full speed, colliding twice, but fortunately without much damage, ere reaching the Cloch. There Price, having established a lead of half a length (due, according to the " Neptune's " crew, to their vessel having a defective float), put about, satisfied, and steamed back to Gourock to resume his regular journey. Of course, an exploit like this required explanation at the River-Bailie Court, where the skippers had to appear on 5th August. Price put up no defence and was fined £5; M'Lean was convicted on evidence and a fine of three guineas imposed. He received a good deal of public sympathy, as it was evident that he had been jockeyed into racing against his inclination. The " Herald " deemed the affair worthy of a " leader," asking, " What right has this man, Price, to entrap people into his vessel for a safe summer-day sail and then subject them to the terror of a violent death by explosion or collision? " It goes on to suggest that "a quiet sixty days in Duke Street prison might bring his romantic notions to some relation with realities."

Price's name disappears after this; probably even the sporting owners of the "Ruby" found him too enterprising; at any rate, the vessel found a new skipper in Charlie Brown, late of the "Rothesay Castle." In 1862 we find her running, not in consort with that vessel, but with the "Neptune," and in June the duplication of the four o'clock service was resumed. If it led to racing —and doubtless it did—no exceptional performances are recorded, and within a week the "Rothesay Castle's" sailing hour was altered to 4.10, in order, as the advertisement put it, to avoid racing. In spite of this, the two old opponents contrived to have a trial of speed on the river on 28th July, with the usual sequel in the River-Bailie Court. Captain M'Intyre of the "Rothesay Castle" was fined three guineas for failing to slow at Renfrew to allow the "Ruby," then the faster vessel, to pass, and Captain Brown was acquitted. Evidently the "Rothesay Castle" had been racing the "Neptune" on the same day, for their skippers were fined for passing Govan ferry at full speed.

It was in the latter part of 1862 that the demand arose for swift steamers to run with goods and munitions into the Confederate ports, blockaded by the Yankees, and the "Ruby" and "Neptune" were promptly picked up for this service, the former taking her departure from Greenock on

15th November. On a trial before leaving the Clyde the " Neptune " ran the lights at a speed of 17.63 knots, so that she was evidently just about as fast as the others. The weather conditions must have been favourable when this run was made, as " bottom foul " is the only reason put forward why a higher speed was not attained. The " Rothesay Castle " followed her rivals in June, 1863, her owners having received the tidy sum of £8500 for her. All three distinguished themselves in their new occupation, the " Ruby " and " Neptune " making a number of successful trips before coming to grief, while the " Rothesay Castle " survived the war, and is traceable for a quarter of a century afterwards, trading on the Canadian Lakes under the name of " Southern Belle."

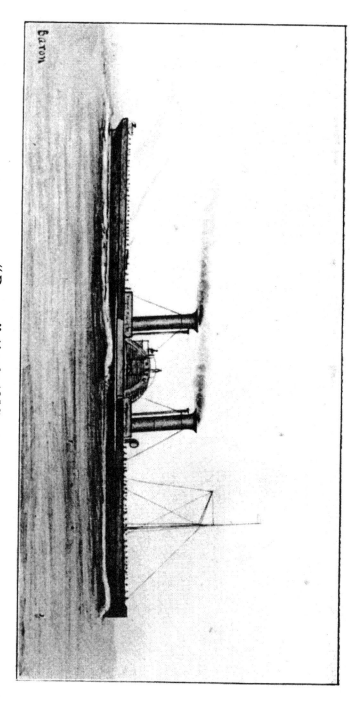

"Baron" (*built 1853*)

Photo. from a Drawing in Mr. Hubbard's collection.

Copied by Messrs. T. & R. Annan & Sons

"Lynx" (*built 1853*), **"Stag"** (*built 1854*)

THE PURCHASES OF THE "EMPEROR OF CHINA"

WHEN President Lincoln, on 19th April, 1861, declared a blockade of all the seaports of the seceding States, the Federal Government was not in possession of a sufficiency of ships to render it effective. For some time the trade of the threatened ports remained unaffected, and vessels arrived and departed without hindrance, but after a lapse of some months Federal gunboats began to make their appearance and some captures were made. It was evident that, if communication with the blockaded ports was to be maintained, special measures would require to be taken. The blockade threatened not only to force the surrender of these ports by cutting off supplies from without, but also, by stopping the export of cotton, to create a famine in that indispensable commodity all over the world. Obviously, if communication could be maintained in spite of the blockade, the enterprise was certain to be lucrative—the inhabitants of the ports, threatened with starvation, would be willing to pay good prices for the necessaries of life, and that not in worthless greenbacks but in honest cotton, for which, in turn, the Lancashire spinners would outbid one another, in order to secure material to keep their machinery going. There was always the risk of losing ship and cargo by capture, but when everything was weighed up the prospects were decidedly bright. All depended on the obtaining of the proper kind of vessels and the proper men to sail them. The blockading ships were not, as a rule, distinguished either for speed or handiness, and the difficulty of their task was increased by the fact that most of the harbours could be entered by several channels. Many of these channels were narrow and winding, strewn with reefs and shoals, and accessible only to handy craft of shallow draught, in the hands of expert local pilots. The pilots were obtainable; their services commanded high prices, but these could easily be afforded from the profits of a successful run, and the attention of the intending blockade-runners was directed to the securing of ships ready to hand for immediate use. Naturally the Clyde's reputation for steamship production attracted them, and by the middle of 1862 we find overtures being made to the owners of fast channel- and river-craft for the purchase of their vessels. The would-be purchasers showed no anxiety to reveal their identity, or the trade for which the vessels were destined; the latter was usually referred to in general terms as the "South American trade," while the purchases were occasionally attributed to "a Spanish firm," or, more frequently, to the "Emperor of China."

Among the first of that potentate's acquisitions were three fast paddle-steamers in the channel trade, the "Leopard," "Herald," and "Adela."

The "Leopard," a vessel of about 700 tons, had been built at Dumbarton by Denny for Messrs. Burns in 1858, and had been plying in their Liverpool service, where she had established herself as a favourite with the travelling public. She had made way for two screw-steamers in 1860, and after a spell on charter to another firm had been offered for sale in the autumn of 1861. The "Herald" was a smaller and older vessel, which had been plying in the Dublin trade for Lewis Potter & Co. for about a dozen years. She would probably have come into the market soon in any case, her owners having a new vessel on the stocks. The "Adela" was a very smart little steamer, built in 1859 by J. & G. Thomson for the Ardrossan-Belfast route, a run which she repeatedly accomplished in 5 hours and 20 minutes. She was constructed on somewhat similar lines to the first "Iona," but a broader and deeper boat. The river-steamer "Pearl" drops out of the advertisements at the end of September in the same year, and, although there is no trace of her sale or departure, subsequent events show that she had gone blockade-running.

The "Iona" had ceased sailing at the middle of September, but as her season would have terminated then in ordinary course little notice was taken of the fact. About a fortnight later, on 2nd October, she sailed down the river, fitted up for a trans-Atlantic voyage, but in Gourock Bay was run down and sunk by a new screw-steamer called

the "Chanticleer," returning from a speed trial.
The "Iona" went down stern foremost half an
hour after being struck, her crew being rescued by
the colliding vessel. Her wreck was advertised for
sale in the following summer, and was actually sold
to a Glasgow man in February, 1863, for £95, but
the purchaser never succeeded in salving her, and
this appears to have given rise to a report that the
whole story of the sinking was merely a ruse to
conceal the fact of her departure. The full report
of the incident, however, published at the time,
just two days after its occurrence, is altogether too
circumstantial to leave room for such an idea.

Before the end of the year the river-fleet had been
further reduced by the departure of the "Eagle,"
"Ruby" and "Dolphin," while of channel-
steamers, the paddle-boats "Giraffe" and "Havelock," and the screws "Fingal," "Tubal Cain,"
"Antona," "Thistle," and "Princess Royal" had
also gone. The "Eagle" had been built by Denny
in 1852 for the Rothesay run, and the "Ruby,"
a very speedy boat, also in the Broomielaw-
Rothesay trade, had come from Henderson's yard
at Renfrew in 1861. The "Dolphin," on the contrary, was an old boat, launched in 1844, and had
been employed for a number of years running with
mails and passengers from Oban to Mull, Staffa,
and Iona, and later on the Glasgow and Inveraray
station. The "Giraffe" had made her appearance
in 1860, being placed on the Greenock and Belfast
route by Messrs. Burns, to make the return journey

between these ports in a single day. Her builders were J. & G. Thomson. This steamer's performances on service had been rather disappointing, but there is no doubt she possessed great speed, as on a preliminary trial-run she covered the distance in 5¾ hours. The " Havelock," also built by Thomson, had been running as a consort to the " Herald " on the Dublin route since 1858, and her performances had stamped her as something above the average in point of speed. Of the screwboats, the " Fingal," one of Hutcheson's West Highland steamers, had only commenced plying in June, 1861; she also was from Thomson's yard. The " Antona " had appeared on the Londonderry run for M'Connell & Laird about the same time. The " Thistle " had been built for Cameron's Londonderry service in 1859 by Laurence Hill & Co., of Port-Glasgow. The " Princess Royal," one of Tod & M'Gregor's productions, had made her first run in Langlands's Liverpool service in July, 1861. The " Tubal Cain " was a small steamer, built at Paisley in 1853 by Blackwood & Gordon, and had figured in various employments.

The " Ruby " and " Giraffe " sailed together from Greenock at the middle of November, but appear to have parted company shortly after leaving the Clyde.

Next to go was the " Neptune," Napier's crack Rothesay boat, turned out in 1861. She sailed from Rothesay on 19th January, 1863.

In the following month news of the doings of

some of the blockade-runners began to reach home, meagre in detail but of considerable interest to those who had known the boats in their home waters. It was learnt that the " Princess Royal " had successfully run the blockade, that the " Giraffe " had arrived at a Southern port, and had brought out a cargo of cotton, but that the " Pearl," " Antona," and " Adela " had fallen into the hands of the Federals. On 9th April news arrived of the capture of the " Princess Royal " and " Thistle." The " Tubal Cain " and " Leopard," too, had met their fate, the former being captured on her first run, and the latter destroyed after eight successful trips. The " Thistle " had only left the Clyde in October, 1862, but had run the blockade repeatedly, bringing her owner a profit of £18,000, after reimbursing him for the £13,800 paid for the vessel. Her first run alone cleared £7000. The " Princess Royal " appears to have got through only once.

The month of May witnessed the departure from the Clyde of the " Juno," the crack boat of M'Kellar's Largs, Millport and Arran fleet, and also that of the latest addition to the Dublin and Glasgow Co.'s fleet, the " Lord Clyde," launched by Caird, of Greenock, only ten months before. The screw-steamer " Tuskar," of the Clyde Shipping Co., also sailed in that month. She had made her début in 1860, Blackwood & Gordon being her builders. The " Tuskar " appears to have been captured at her first attempt.

In June the "Spunkie" went off. This was one of a pair of fast steamers which Tod & M'Gregor had placed on the Largs and Millport station in 1857. Her sister-ship, the "Kelpie," transferred in her second season to the Shannon, had joined the "Imperial" service in 1862, but had come to grief in the same year. A steamer building to replace the "Eagle" was bought on the stocks at Connell's, received the name of "Mary Anne," and after a trial-trip, in the course of which a speed of 19 miles an hour was realised, despatched to Nassau on 23rd June. She made seven successful trips before falling into the blockaders' hands. Two paddle-steamers, the "Roe" and the "Fox," building at Caird's for Burns's Belfast trade, also changed hands while in course of construction, other two vessels to replace them in the Burns fleet being laid down in the vacant berths immediately they were launched.

At the end of June Simons's "Rothesay Castle," the last of the three fliers whose performances had enlivened the Rothesay route in 1861 and 1862, was sold for £8500. She made her last run to Rothesay on 1st July, being replaced next day by the "Hero," a former Clyde steamer, brought back from Belfast Lough, where she had been employed for a couple of seasons. The "Mail," the crack boat of the Kilmun station, owned by Captain Campbell, who had got her from Tod & M'Gregor in 1860, and the "Jupiter," consort to the "Juno" in M'Kellar's fleet, went away in July. The two

M'Kellar boats had also come from the Partick yard, the " Jupiter " in 1856 and her consort in 1860. Their owner probably welcomed the opportunity to dispose of them at a good price, as the impending opening of the Wemyss-Bay Railway rendered the prospects of the trade from the Broomielaw to Largs and Millport very precarious. The August departures included the " Rothesay Castle," already mentioned; the " Gem," built by J Henderson & Sons at Renfrew in 1854, to run to Helensburgh and Garelochhead, but which had latterly been sailing to Rothesay; the " Scotia," an old steamer on the Ayr and Campbeltown run; and a steamer called the " Diamond." The last-named had been bought by Messrs. Henderson on the Neva, where she had been plying, and brought over to the Clyde to replace the boats they had sold. The price paid for her was £4000, but before she had been placed on the river her new owners accepted the " Emperor's " offer of £7500 for her, and she was promptly fitted out for his service. It has been repeatedly stated that this vessel was originally the " Baron," which sailed on the Glasgow and Rothesay run between 1854 and 1857, but as that steamer was sent to Havre in the latter year, and is still traceable in Lloyd's Register nearly thirty years later as the " Normandie," French-owned, and with no indication of having ever borne any previous name except " Baron," it scarcely seems likely that the " Diamond " can have been the same vessel.

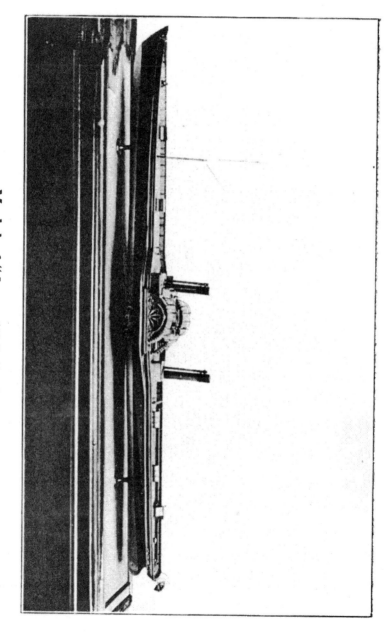

Model of "Iona (1)" (*built 1855*)

"Gairlochy" (*built 1861*)

Another of M'Kellar's boats left in September, the " Star." Her builders were Tod & M'Gregor, but she was an older boat than the " Jupiter " and the " Juno "; nevertheless, in her new occupation she proved the most successful of the three. After leaving Queenstown this steamer had to put back, leaky, and discharge there for repairs; the " Rothesay Castle," too, returned to that port with a damaged paddle-box, but both eventually crossed the Atlantic all right. An interesting item in the shipping news of 6th August might readily pass unnoticed. It is in these words :—" Queenstown, 5th Aug., sailed, ' Alliance ' (s), Liverpool for Nassau." This was Mills's unsuccessful double-hulled boat, described in a previous chapter.

News had come home at the end of July that the " Herald " had made a successful run from Nassau to Charleston, but a message received on 19th October announced her capture by the Federals. By that time she must have paid her cost over and over again, having eluded the blockading fleet on no fewer than 28 occasions. The " Neptune " had failed to escape from the blockaders in May, after several profitable trips. The " Jupiter " was less fortunate. Little more than two months after leaving Greenock she was " hors de combat." It was also reported that the " Mail " had been set on fire by her skipper, lest her cargo should fall into the hands of the Federals, but this must have been erroneous, as, though the Federals eventually got her, it was not till the autumn of 1864, by which time she had no doubt had ample opportunities of making money for her owners. The "Giraffe" and "Spunkie" were reported to be working with great success. The former, which had been renamed "Robert E. Lee," had made Halifax her headquarters, and was running in and out of Wilmington, her weatherly qualities suiting her well for this long trip in exposed waters. The blockade of Charleston was by that time so closely maintained that the run thither from Nassau could only be made with much difficulty and risk. But the pitcher went once too often to the well. According to a despatch received on 28th November, the old Belfast boat had been fired on and struck, on a run from Wilmington to Halifax, in September, but her speed had saved her, though her hull was damaged and three of her crew wounded. Of course, her speed was her only defence, as a single shot fired by a blockade-runner would have been an act of piracy, and have exposed her crew, in the event of subsequent capture, to the unpleasant treatment meted out to pirates. The steamer left Halifax again on 22nd October, but the people of Wilmington were left vainly "waiting for the 'R. E. Lee,'" for on this trip she was captured by a cruiser. The "Adela" is again heard of, this time in the rôle of a Federal cruiser in Tampa Bay, where, in company with a consort, she captured and destroyed two vessels attempting to enter the port.

On Christmas day the "Caledonia," a paddle-

steamer which had been running to Ayr, set out
to cross the Atlantic, and five days later the second
"Iona," built to replace the one which had been
sold and lost in the previous year, went down the
river, stripped of her saloons and painted light
grey. This was a measure adopted with all the
blockade-runners to render them difficult of detec-
tion against the land. The precaution was even
taken of dressing the crew in garments of a similar
inconspicuous hue. Coal as nearly smokeless as
could be obtained was burnt, and on occasion the
paddle-floats were muffled. Running the lights
on 30th December, the "Iona" is said to have
attained a speed of twenty-one miles an hour,
which was probably within her powers, but which
would be more convincing without the claim that
it was done "under easy steaming" and against
wind and tide. One is inclined to ask why they
did not run the lights in the opposite direction
and "let her rip." Her final departure from the
Clyde well loaded with coals took place on 18th
January, 1864, and she lay at Queenstown till the
end of the month, insubordination having broken
out among her crew, thirteen of whom refused to
proceed to sea in her. Their reluctance was justified when bad weather was encountered shortly
after leaving Queenstown and the vessel sprang
a leak, the water entering faster than the pumps
could cope with it, so that the captain found himself compelled to put about and run for Milford
Haven. Before she could get there he had to

abandon her, the stokehold being drowned out and the engines stopped, and half an hour afterwards the " Iona " foundered. It has been stated, probably through carelessness, that she was lost with all hands. Fortunately the affair was not so tragic, the crew being all landed at Ilfracombe safe and sound.

Among the last boats picked up for the " South American trade " were a paddle-boat of Cameron's 'Derry fleet, the " Thistle," only a few months old, built to replace the screw-steamer of the same name which had gone blockade-running in 1862, and the " Fairy," also a paddle-steamer, built by Thomson in 1862 to ply on the Caledonian Canal, the first saloon-steamer in the Hutcheson fleet. By this time a number of boats had been built specially for the requirements of this exceptional trade; the increased stringency of the blockade had rendered the nearer ports almost inaccessible, and something more substantial than an ordinary river-steamer was required to face the longer and stormier routes to such ports as could still be entered.

Among the most successful of the Clyde boats engaged in the enterprise were the " Herald," which, as already stated, made 28 trips, the " Lord Clyde " (18 trips), the " Havelock " and " Giraffe " (14 each), "Leopard" (8), "Ruby" (7), "Spunkie" and " Eagle " (6 each), " Scotia " (5), " Star " and " Rothesay Castle." The number of trips accomplished by the two last-named is not available, but it must have been very considerable, as neither was ever captured. All the others mentioned in this list were either captured, sunk or destroyed. The " Eagle," captured and sold, resumed the old game, and carried a cotton cargo from Galveston, Texas, to Tampico, in Mexico, just before the close of the war. After the war the " Rothesay Castle " was sent to the Canadian lakes, where she sailed for a very long time; the " Star " remained at Nassau, and is there to this day. The case of the " Dolphin " is a strange one. According to a letter purporting to be signed by her owner, and published in April, 1863, she was seized by a Federal vessel on her outward voyage to Nassau, when off the Danish island of St. Thomas, where she had called to replenish her coal supply. If the facts are as stated in the letter the Yankee skipper's action was very high-handed, as the steamer was bound from one British port to another; but, as nothing more is heard of the incident, the suspicion arises that there may have been some details of the affair which the writer has not thought fit to emphasise. The " Dolphin " was sold in New York in the summer of 1864, and went back to blockade-running, in which occupation she was captured off Key West on 27th February, 1865, bearing the name of " Ruby."

Word arrived in April, 1864, that the " Juno " had foundered in a storm and taken part of her crew to the bottom with her. The capture of the " Lord Clyde," " Diamond " and " Scotia," and the destruction of the " Havelock " were reported about the same time. It was also reported that the " Gem " had been lost, but this seems to have been untrue, as according to later reports she was still running. The " Alliance " was captured at Savannah in April, 1864, after several successful trips, and was afterwards auctioned at New York, finding her way eventually to New Zealand, where her career was ended by stranding in August, 1865. Following the " Alliance," the " Caledonia," " Fairy " and paddle " Thistle " were soon captured. The former " Thistle," screw-boat, had now become the U.S. Blockade-watcher " Cherokee," and distinguished herself by the seizure of the new paddle blockade-runner "Emma Hendry."

There may have been other Clyde steamers engaged in blockade-running, whose names have not been mentioned. The " Craignish Castle," for example, was in the market in May, 1862, and is not advertised to sail after that year. It is said, and may well be true, that she went into the " South American trade," but there is no trace of her in the newspaper reports from the other side. Likely enough she came to grief on the passage out, a fate which befell the first " Chancellor," despatched from the Clyde for blockade-running in the summer of 1863.

The details given are all from contemporary sources, which should, naturally, be the most reliable, yet even the accuracy of these is not always to be implicitly depended on. For instance,

"Neptune" (*built 1861*)

one account stated that the " Vesta " and " Hero " had gone off across the Atlantic, and that the " Vulcan " was about to follow. None of these boats left the Clyde, and yet, in a trans-Atlantic message, received on 30th January, 1864, the capture was announced of " the Arran, Rothesay and Glasgow steamer ' Hero,' when attempting to enter a blockaded port," whereas, at that time, the steamer was plying regularly between Glasgow and Rothesay. Probably this was a case of mistaken identity; the name of " Hero " may well have been given to some old Clyde favourite in trans-Atlantic waters, in which case confusion might naturally arise.

A similar incident occurred in connection with the Belfast steamer " Lynx," which was plying on her regular station when word came home that she had been destroyed at Wilmington—but in this instance it was evident that the vessel which had suffered the mishap was a Liverpool-built steamer of the same name.

In spite of all the " Emperor of China's " purchases, an astonishingly good steamboat service was maintained on the Firth during the summer of 1863, the only time when there was any inconvenience from shortage of boats being the Glasgow Fair week, when some of the channel-steamers were placed in excursion work on the Firth for a day or two. By the following summer a number of new boats had appeared, sufficient to meet all the demands of the coast traffic.

THE EARLY DAYS OF THE
WEMYSS BAY ROUTE

IN November, 1862, operations were commenced on the construction of the Greenock and Wemyss Bay Railway. The line was a single one, extending from Port-Glasgow to Wemyss Bay by way of Upper Greenock, and its object was to provide a more rapid means of communication between Glasgow and a number of the watering-places on the Firth, particularly Rothesay, Millport and Largs, than was afforded by the existing Glasgow and Greenock Railway, or the river route from the Broomielaw. The employment of fast boats on the Rothesay station had on occasions reduced the time occupied on the journey to two and a half hours by steamer all the way, or two hours by rail and steamer, but such cases were exceptional, and evidently represented the fastest that it was possible to hope for by these routes. The increased proportion of railway travelling and short water-passage by the Wemyss Bay route were confidently expected to enable the journey to be made in less time. On the Largs and Millport station the advantage seemed likely to be even more marked. The trade to these places was then, and had been for many years, maintained by the steamers of the M'Kellar fleet. Some of these were good boats of recent construction, but others were rather antiquated, and none of them had the great speed which competition had called forth in the case of the Rothesay boats, so that an efficient service of fast trains and up-to-date steamers via Wemyss Bay seemed assured of success.

The Wemyss Bay Steamboat Co. was formed, to work in connection with the railway, and contracts were placed for three paddle-steamers, two with Caird & Co., of Greenock, and one with Thomas Wingate & Co., of Glasgow. The former were expensive vessels, superior in size and comfort to any contemporary river-boat save the " Iona," smart-looking two-funnelled steamers with deck saloons fore and aft, and fitted with powerful oscillating engines, intended to give them a speed of nineteen miles an hour. The Wingate boat was intended for all-the-year-round work, and was smaller than the other two, which were essentially summer-boats. Her main deck was flush, and she had a long hurricane-deck over the engine-house and boilers. Her engines were of a new diagonal oscillating type, designed by her builders, but no such speed was aimed at as in the case of the Caird boats. Like them, she was two-funnelled.

The first of the three was launched from the Greenock yard on 17th August, 1864, but she had already been sold for blockade-running, and under the name of " Hattie " she ran her trials on 1st November, and is said to have attained the contract speed. Eight days later the "Hattie" sailed for Nassau, arriving out just in time to come to grief before the end of the war. A sister-ship, to replace her in the Wemyss Bay fleet, was laid down in the vacant berth immediately after the launch.

The "Largs," as the steamer built by Wingate was called, left the ways on Saturday, 17th September, and just four weeks later the second Caird boat, the "Kyles," was launched at Greenock, but their completion was not hurried, as there was no prospect of the railway being opened before the summer.

The proprietors of the M'Kellar boats, realising that the opening of the new railway was bound to hurt their trade, had availed themselves of the demand for blockade-runners to dispose of three of their vessels at good prices, while a fourth had been bought by another Clyde owner for the Broomielaw-Rothesay trade, to replace his own steamer gone to Nassau. The M'Kellar fleet was thus reduced from seven vessels to three, and as two of the steamers sold were the newest and fastest of the lot its efficiency was even more impaired than the reduction in numbers would suggest. The Largs and Millport service had to be cut down in a manner which caused much dis-satisfaction in these watering-places, and numerous letters complaining of its inadequacy appeared in the newspapers during the summer of 1864. Not only were the boats old and slow, but their upkeep had been neglected so badly that about the end of August a strongly-worded letter was published, signed by John Burns and other twenty-two prominent Glasgow men, protesting against their disgraceful condition, more especially that of the steamer " Lady Kelburne," and the remissness of the Board of Trade surveyor in allowing them to sail. The condition of the " Lady Kelburne " may be inferred from the fact that when she was put up for auction, towards the end of 1866, the reserve price was only £400.

Such a state of affairs was all in favour of the start of the new enterprise, and at the beginning of April, 1865, at the opening of the spring season, the Wemyss Bay Steamboat Co. seized the opportunity to place the " Largs " on a daily run from the Broomielaw to Largs, Fairlie, and Millport until the new railway should be opened, an event which was expected to take place in about six weeks. This move, as it was meant to do, attracted a good deal of attention, and a week later a newspaper paragraph appeared, stating that the new steamer was giving great satisfaction and proving herself very fast and a good sea-boat.

Weatherly and comfortable she doubtless was, but the scribe who extolled her speed was surely drawing on his imagination, as the " Largs " neither was nor was designed to be anything exceptional in that regard, and he must have felt rather foolish when, one day about the middle of June, the thirteen-year-old " Venus," of the despised M'Kellar fleet, left Millport pier astern of the new steamer and showed her the way to Largs. Great disappointment was felt when the "Kyles," running the lights on 29th April, failed to exceed $17\frac{1}{2}$ miles an hour, and, although another trial ten days later gave better results, her performance still fell half a mile below the contract speed.

The Government inspection of the Wemyss Bay Railway took place on 27th April with satisfactory results. A specially-invited party of 600 guests travelled to Wemyss Bay by the new line on 12th May, and on the following day another party proceeded to Wemyss Bay by rail, joining the "Kyles" there and sailing to Lamlash.

The regular service was immediately commenced and the two boats were kept very fully employed. The "Kyles" lay overnight at Tighnabruaich, sailing thence at 6.40 a.m. for Wemyss Bay via Rothesay, returning to Rothesay in time to make another trip from that port to Wemyss Bay at 9.25. There she connected with the 8.40 train from Bridge Street, getting to Rothesay in time to sail again for Wemyss Bay at 10.45. On the arrival of the 10.45 train she started off for Rothesay and Tighnabruaich, leaving the latter port again at 2 p.m., and retracing her way to Wemyss Bay for another trip to Rothesay in connection with the train leaving Glasgow at 3.50. Leaving Rothesay again at 5.45, she met the 5 o'clock train at Wemyss Bay and completed her day with a run to Rothesay and Tighnabruaich.

The "Largs" had her overnight quarters at Lamlash, whence she sailed each morning for Wemyss Bay at 5.30, calling at Millport and Largs. Thereafter she made three journeys to Millport, the first one empty, and the others in connection with the 8.40 and 10.45 trains, returning from Millport at 9 and 11 a.m. and 2.45 p.m., and from Largs half an hour later. On the 3.50 connection she proceeded to Largs only, returning direct to Wemyss Bay to connect with the 5 o'clock train for a final run to Largs, Millport and Lamlash.

In the beginning of June, Innellan and Dunoon were added to the ports served from Wemyss Bay. To enable this additional traffic to be overtaken, a steamer called the "Victory" was bought in and added to the company's fleet. This was an economical boat of fair speed and good passenger accommodation, built for the Broomielaw-Rothesay trade, in which she had been plying for a couple of years for Captain Duncan Stewart.

To maintain the daily programme of sailings as set forth in the schedule would have taxed the most efficient management, even with perfect punctuality on the part of trains and steamers; it allowed no margin for making up lost time, and was liable to be completely upset by any unforeseen delay. Unfortunately such delays were of only too common occurrence; the steamers' lack of speed and the difficulty of working the single-line railway, which on one occasion was completely blocked for a whole day owing to a sudden fall of rock, were fruitful causes of detention, so that the frequent disorganisation of the traffic produced many a bitter complaint from passengers and earned for the Wemyss Bay route a reputation for unpunctuality that augured but ill for its success. The "Bute," a sister-ship to the "Kyles," joined the fleet about midsummer, and had the company been content to adhere to the existing time-table the addition of this fine vessel might well have enabled an efficient service to be given, but no sooner had she appeared on the station than additional sailings were announced. Ardrishaig was added to the ports served from Wemyss Bay, and, not content with maintaining the railway connections, the company established two sailings daily from the Broomielaw. The "Bute" started thence each morning at half-past eight for Arran, while the "Kyles" came up the river in the forenoon and left again for Ardrishaig at half-past two.

The Ardrishaig venture was an utter failure and lasted only a fortnight, and by the end of August the Broomielaw sailings were altogether discontinued.

A month later a much-reduced winter service came into operation, only the "Victory" and the "Largs" being employed, and the two saloon boats withdrawn. They were not destined to reappear in the Firth trade, being sold to London owners and despatched to the Thames in January, 1866. The "Bute," renamed "Princess Alice," ended her days in tragic fashion in September, 1878, being

sunk by collision, with frightful loss of life. The
" Kyles," to which the name of " Albert Edward "
had been given, survived her on the Thames for
many years.

Before the opening of the summer season of
1866 the " Argyle," a new steamer built for Captain Stewart to replace the " Victory," which she
closely resembled, was bought in. When the
Wemyss Bay Co. got her, she had only been plying
for three weeks. The summer time-table was
modified to adapt it to the capabilities of the three
boats; the Broomielaw sailings were not resumed,
the connections to the more distant places were
dropped, and attention concentrated on the traffic
on the Rothesay and Millport sections. Certainly
complaints of unpunctuality were far less frequent
than in the preceding season.

A flat fare of one shilling was established, for
which a passenger could travel from any one port
on the steamboat system to any other and back.
Had a similar broad-minded policy characterised
more of the company's dealings, popularity, and
with it success, would probably have been secured,
but the directors seem to have been unfortunate
in arousing popular resentment over small irrita-
tions. For instance, they refused to issue through-
tickets on board the boats to any destination save
Glasgow, and imposed a pier-tax at Wemyss Bay
on all who were unable to produce such; sometimes, too, they withdrew steamboat connections
on very inadequate notice, quite failing to realise

(Victory) marquis of Lorne) Cumbrae)

"**Victory**" (*built 1863*)

"Largs" (*built 1864*)

Photo. by Messrs. G. W. Wilson & Co., Aberdeen (now Mr. Fred J. Hardie)

how much inconvenience and loss were sure to be occasioned thereby.

The Railway Company at least paid something to the preference shareholders, but the Steamboat Company was a losing concern from the start. Even with the disposal of the extravagant saloon-boats and the substitution of the economical " Victory " and " Argyle," it could not make ends meet; each year's working showed a loss, and in 1869 it found itself unable to carry on any longer. The " Victory " was got rid of, and went back to the up-river trade, and the Railway Company eventually came to an arrangement with Messrs. Campbell & Gillies, who took over the " Argyle " and " Largs," to which they added the " Venus," acquired when Captain M'Kellar went out of business. Being good business men, thoroughly versed in the coast passenger-trade, they soon had the steamers running at a profit, and continued to maintain the service until the Caledonian Railway Co. acquired the Wemyss Bay Railway, and entrusted the steamboat connections to the Caledonian Steam-Packet Co.

IN THE OUTER WATERS

A STRIKING feature in the history of the Clyde river-boats is the hardiness which many of them have exhibited under conditions far more severe than were contemplated in their construction. Their success as channel transports and as mine-sweepers in exposed waters during the recent Great War was phenomenal; such losses as occurred were all due to enemy action or collision; not a single one of the steamers succumbed to stress of weather. Of the boats of an older generation, sent across the Atlantic for blockade-running, only one or two failed to accomplish the voyage in safety, and not a few old Clyde favourites have been seen in such distant quarters as Australia and South America, having made their way thither on their own bottoms. The machinery, in several instances, was removed and sent out separately, the hulls, temporarily strengthened and rigged, making the voyage under canvas. Unlikely as it might appear, more than one of them proved handy craft under the altered conditions, and it is recorded that the "Breadalbane," an old Loch Goil boat, expatriated in 1853, sailed so well under schooner-rig that most of the small craft she encountered on the way gave her as wide a berth as possible, convinced that the long, low, raking hull, cleaving the water so rapidly, could only belong to some pirate craft. The " Glasgow Citizen," too, after a season or two in the Rothesay trade, followed the " Breadalbane " to the Antipodes, similarly transformed. On the way out she fell in with a sailing-ship bound in the same direction, whose master promised to report the little vessel on his arrival at Melbourne, but was surprised to find, on getting out, that she had not only outsailed him, but was already re-converted into a steamer and engaged in trading there. But the ocean got the " Glasgow Citizen " at last, for, after plying eight or nine years on the Australian coast, she left Melbourne for Otago on 11th October, 1862, and disappeared, and only the picking-up of part of one of her name-boards on the eastern coast of New Zealand six months afterwards furnished any clue to her fate.

But not all the steamers sold overseas were fortunate enough to reach their new ports of hail in safety, and the waters and coasts of the Channel can tell of quite a number, especially of those sent off in winter time, that met their fate by foundering or being driven ashore within a few days or even hours after leaving the shelter of the Clyde.

One of these was the " Eva," which was sold to Australian owners about the same time as the " Breadalbane " and " Glasgow Citizen." She was a small steamer which had plied for a single season on the Dunoon and Holy Loch route, in connection with the Greenock railway. Leaving the Clyde under canvas on 27th December, 1853, she encountered a storm off Lambay Island, which caused her to break in two and founder, taking ten of her crew to the bottom with her.

The "Osprey," a big, powerful boat, built by Barclay, Curle & Co. for the Rothesay station in 1852, was sold to West Indian owners at the end of her second season, and never heard of after sailing.

The "Koh-i-Noor," built in 1852, sailed for a couple of seasons in the Strone and Kilmun trade from the Broomielaw. After that she was chartered to run between Limerick and Kilrush, on the Shannon estuary. When the charter expired, a tug was sent round to Limerick to bring her back to the Clyde, and on 16th March, 1855, the tow started in fine weather. The following day, the wind freshening to a gale with a heavy sea caused the hawser to carry away the fore-bulwarks of the "Koh-i-Noor." This gave the hawser so much play that the vessel would not steer and repeatedly broached-to, while the sea gradually filled her. The crew were forced to take to the lifeboat, and the tug, casting-off the "Koh-i-Noor," steamed after them and picked them up. By the time this was done the storm had reached such a height that further assistance to the "Koh-i-Noor" was impossible; the tug, with both crews aboard, was compelled to abandon her and seek safety in the shelter of Broadhaven.

As mentioned elsewhere, the "Windsor Castle"

of 1859 and the second " Ruby " were despatched
under canvas in the autumn of 1860, their destination being an Indian port, but their voyages were
over as soon as begun, the one vessel being driven
ashore at Sanda and the other on the County Down
coast, while the " Iona " (second of the name),
bound for Nassau, foundered off Lundy Island
in the beginning of February, 1864.

A handsome two-funnelled steamer, of dimensions and design very similar to those of the first
" Iona," was laid down by Kirkpatrick, M'Intyre
& Co., of Port-Glasgow, in 1864, with a view to
being sold for blockade-running, but by the time
she was ready for sea the trade offered no remunera-
tive employment for vessels of her class. She was
bought by Captain Watson, formerly owner of the
fast " Rothesay Castle " No. 4, and was placed by
him on the Rothesay station, under the name of
" Arran Castle," in August, 1864. For the
remainder of that season and during the whole of
the following one she remained in the Rothesay
trade, proving a great favourite with the public.
Her speed was above the average; on a trial-trip
at the end of April, 1865, immediately before the
start of her second season, the " lights " were run
in 48 minutes, or at a rate of 17 knots. In January,
1866, we find her running on charter for the
Wemyss Bay Co. while one of their vessels was
receiving an overhaul, and that appears to have
been her last service on the Clyde. Competition
on the Firth of Clyde was keen, and fares were cut

too low to admit of much margin of profit, and the owner of the " Arran Castle," judging that the Thames offered better prospects, determined to take his steamer thither and ply with her between London and Gravesend. The " Arran Castle " had originally been flush-decked, but in order to render her more attractive to the Londoners, Captain Watson had her fitted with a large deck-saloon. The alterations being completed, she steamed down the river on 21st March, and after adjusting compasses, set forth on a voyage which she was expected to perform in about sixty hours. On board of her were the owner and his son, a boy of eleven years, her commander, Captain Brown, two brothers named Campbell, who acted as stewards, a Mr. Wighton of Glasgow, and a crew of 15 deck-hands, engineers, firemen and trimmers. One of the Clyde Shipping Co.'s steamers passed her at 10 o'clock on the morning of the 22nd, some distance north of Dublin; weather fine and all well. Later on the same day she was seen from another steamer north of Wicklow light. But no word came of her arrival at her destination, and on the morning of the 29th the coasting steamer "Jasper" arrived at Greenock, bringing with her some pieces of wreckage picked up between Portpatrick and Corsewall, which were recognised as part of the fittings of the " Arran Castle." Other arrivals brought more wreckage and reported that great quantities of it were floating off the Wigtownshire coast. The weather in the Channel, fine when the

"Arran Castle" was last seen, was known to have changed suddenly that evening, bringing with it a violent storm, under stress of which, it was conjectured, the vessel had put back, only to be overwhelmed near the Mull of Galloway. The quantity of wreckage found floating was regarded by many people as an indication that the disaster had been due to the bursting of the boilers rather than to foundering. It seems most likely that she foundered through stress of weather, her boilers exploding as she went down, but nothing more than the wreckage told was ever known of the fate of the ship or of those aboard her.

In the same year that produced the "Arran Castle," two very small steamers, the "Leven" and the "Lennox," were launched by the Clyde Shipbuilding Co. to revive the passenger trade to Dumbarton, which had been allowed to lapse for some years. They measured only 140 feet by 14 feet, and were driven by tiny oscillating engines of 40 horse-power. The "Leven" started plying on the last day of May, 1864, the "Lennox" joining her fully a fortnight later, and the two boats remained on the station till 27th December, 1866. Three days before their withdrawal a paragraph had appeared, stating that they had been sold to the Bahia Steam Navigation Co. for service in Brazil.

Three weeks earlier the same firm had purchased the "Vesper," the latest addition to Captain Campbell's Kilmun fleet, a vessel of raised-quarterdeck

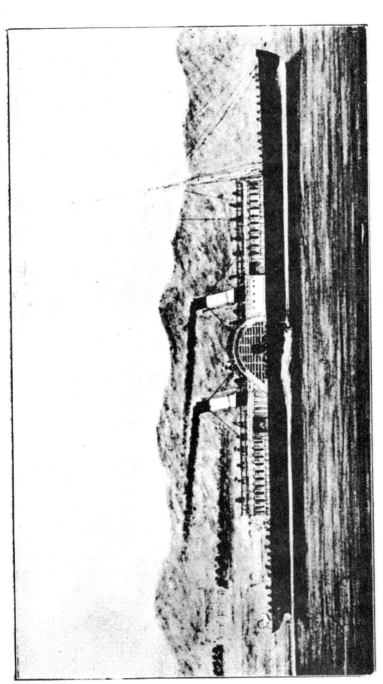

"Bute" (*built 1865*)

Photo, from a Drawing in Mr. Hubbard's Collection

design, with a steeple-engine removed from one of
his earlier steamers. The "Vesper," which was
considerably larger than the Dumbarton boats,
measuring 175 feet by 17 feet, had only been
plying for six months.

Preparatory to sailing, the three vessels received
Portuguese names, and were rigged as schooners,
while their paddles and probably their machinery
were removed, though the paddle-wings were
allowed to remain. The attempt to sail them to
Brazil was a complete fiasco. The "Vesper," renamed "Leitao Cunha," set out on 3rd January,
only to founder off St. Ives on the 19th. The
departure of the "Sevaros," ex "Leven," took
place on 8th March. On the 13th she put into
Loch Ryan, storm-stayed, and on the 20th was
abandoned in a sinking condition off the Irish
coast, her crew being picked up by a passing vessel.
She outlasted by three days her sister-ship, the
"Lennox," which, bearing the name of "Taviros
Bastor," had left Greenock two days after her, and
which had gone ashore near Kingstown on the 17th
and become a total wreck. Three boats less fitted
for an ocean voyage could scarcely have been
selected from among the Clyde fleet, and it may
have been their crews' good fortune that they
encountered heavy weather so near home and never
were called upon to face the Atlantic.

Less fortunate in this respect was the "Guinevere," long a favourite boat on the Arran route.
She was considerably larger than any of those just

mentioned, but not by any means the sort of vessel that one would choose for a voyage in exposed waters. After more than twenty years' service on the Clyde she was purchased by a firm in Constantinople. Her end, which came about in a hurricane in the Bay of Biscay, was witnessed by the crew of a Clan liner, under circumstances which rendered any help impossible.

THE ROCKY ROAD TO DUBLIN

In 1862 the Dublin and Glasgow Steam Packet Co. sold their two steamers, the "Herald" and the "Havelock," for blockade-running purposes. At the time the sale was effected they had two new steamers building with Caird & Co., and in order that the Dublin service might not lapse the departure of the "Havelock" was delayed until one of these, the "Lord Clyde," had taken her place on the station. This she did in September. The new vessel acquitted herself well, and in the course of the following month was reported to have established a new record by running from Greenock to Dublin in twelve hours and a quarter, the best passage up to that time being one of thirteen hours and ten minutes by the "Havelock" in 1859. As a consort to the "Lord Clyde" the company chartered the "Vanguard," which they had sold out of their service some time before. This steamer, built by Robert Napier in 1843, is regarded even yet as one of the best-constructed iron ships ever launched, but the increasing importance of the Dublin trade called for larger and speedier vessels. The "Lord Clyde" had only been running for about six months when her owners accepted a tempting offer for her, and like her predecessors she went into the " South American trade," an occupation in which all three achieved remarkable success.

Meantime the owners of the "Vanguard" having sold her to an East Coast firm, her charter came to an end. The "Lord Clyde" made her last trip to Dublin on 13th May, 1863, and for a month after that the service was maintained by various odd boats, chartered as opportunity presented itself. The second of the new Caird boats, the "Lord Gough," took up her station in the middle of June, her maiden run being accomplished in 12 hours 16 minutes. A new "Lord Clyde" had been laid down when the original vessel of the name was sold; her construction was hastened with such energy that her launch took place on 24th October, and in the first week of the new year she was sailing on the Dublin station. A run of 12 hours 40 minutes, from Dublin to Greenock, made a few days later is described, unaccountably enough, as "unprecedentedly short," and "nearly an hour shorter than the fastest passages of the first 'Lord Clyde' or the present steamer the 'Lord Gough.'"

Three months later the fleet was strengthened by the addition of another steamer, the "Earl of Carlisle," also from Caird's yard, which succeeded in lowering the record on her first trip at the middle of April. Her time from Greenock to Dublin is given by the Dublin correspondent of "The Glasgow Herald" as 12 hours 4 minutes

and by "The Irish Times" as 11 hours
57 minutes.

These three vessels were sister-ships, handsome
paddle-boats of about 750 tons, with oscillating
engines of 300 horse-power. They were schooner-
rigged, with bowsprits and figureheads, and each
had two black funnels perched behind a pair of
huge paddle-boxes. All three acquired rather
sinister reputations for colliding with other vessels,
the waters in the neighbourhood of Greenock
appearing to have a strange fatality for them. The
running-down of a schooner off Greenock by the
"Lord Gough" on 1st November, 1864, resulted
in the death of four men, and the sinking of the
little steamer "Guy Fawkes" by the "Earl of
Carlisle" almost at the same spot, eight weeks
afterwards, cost the lives of a similar number.
These are but two of many mishaps in which the
Dublin steamers were concerned, although probably two of the most tragic.

With these three vessels a service of four sailings
weekly in either direction was maintained throughout 1864, 1865, and 1866. In the latter year,
however, the company decided to add another
vessel to their fleet with the object of establishing
a daily service. This time the contract for the hull
was placed with Messrs. Robert Duncan & Co.,
of Port-Glasgow, Messrs. Rankin & Blackmore
being commissioned to supply the engines.

In April, 1866, the "Earl of Dublin" (building) is added to the list of steamers in the com-

pany's advertisement. The launch of the new
steamer, which was similar in dimensions and
power, and doubtless also in design, to the other
boats, took place on 27th November, but it was
not till the beginning of March, 1867, that she was
placed in service. On her maiden trip she just
succeeded in lowering the record with a run of
11 hours 55 minutes from Greenock. It was the
sole opportunity she had, as on her second trip she
went ashore on the County Down coast at Bally-
halbert. Passengers and crew were got off safely,
but the steamer's position was recognised to be
critical, although with fine weather there was some
hope of refloating her. Unfortunately a storm
arose, and the " Earl of Dublin " was so badly
mauled that the owners abandoned her to the
underwriters. The wreck was auctioned at Belfast
on 1st May and purchased by Messrs. Harland &
Wolff of that city. The purchasers succeeded in
salving the engines and boilers as well as the forward part of the hull and some portions of the
after-part. The hull was rebuilt at Belfast, and at
the same time lengthened by some 25 feet. It was
then sent over to Greenock, whither the engines
had preceded it, to be overhauled by Messrs.
Rankin & Blackmore, by whom they were refitted,
the " Earl of Dublin " leaving their hands in the
summer of 1868 as good as new and looking hand-
somer than ever. On a trial-trip on Belfast Lough
the reconstructed vessel rammed and upset a pile
lighthouse, but without herself sustaining any

damage, and fortunately the lighthouse-keeper, his wife and child were rescued, though not without difficulty.

When compelled to abandon their steamer to the underwriters, the Dublin and Glasgow Steam Packet Co. immediately began looking about for a suitable vessel to replace her. A Liverpool firm, trading between that port and Dublin, had given up business in the preceding year, and their three paddle-steamers were still in the market. The largest of these, the " Great Northern," built at Kirkcaldy in 1864, was bought by the Dublin and Glasgow Steam Packet Co. She was rather larger than their own boats and of equal power, and required but slight alterations to fit her for their service. As soon as these were effected she was placed on the Glasgow and Dublin station as the "Marquis of Abercorn." Her speed was probably scarcely equal to that of her consorts, as no exceptional runs of hers are recorded, but her fine accommodation for cattle rendered her a very suitable boat for the trade. Her career with her new owners was short, however, lasting less than two years and ending disastrously. On 17th May, 1869, she collided with her consort, the " Lord Gough," near Portpatrick, and went to the bottom, taking with her 200 head of cattle, though fortunately the colliding steamer, which was comparatively little damaged, succeeded in taking off the crew and passengers.

Negotiations were at once entered into for the repurchase of the " Earl of Dublin," and very

soon her name reappears in the Dublin and
Glasgow Co.'s advertisement. A few days later,
however, it is replaced by the name "Duke of
Edinburgh," which it had been decided to confer
on the repurchased steamer, partly, perhaps, in
order to avoid emphasising her identity, and partly
in compliment to the Duke, who was prominently
in the public eye at the time. Her speed does not
appear to have been improved, as a run of thirteen
hours ten minutes is recorded as something exceptional.

If the change of name was intended to avert
ill fortune, it failed entirely of its object, for in
little more than four months after her reappearance
in the Dublin and Glasgow Co.'s fleet this ill-
starred vessel was ashore again, and destined to
become a total wreck. Homeward bound from
Dublin on the morning of 19th January, 1870,
she rammed Ailsa Craig at full speed. Patches of
mist were lying on the water at the time, and one
of these had so closely resembled the appearance
of the Craig as to deceive both the lookout and
the officers on duty, while another patch completely
hid the rock itself. Attempts were made to refloat
the vessel, the steamer "Raven" from Liverpool
coming alongside and endeavouring to tow her off,
but the speed at which the "Duke" had been
travelling when she went on had fixed her too
firmly, the hawsers broke, and the attempt had to
be abandoned. Captain Coppin, of Londonderry,
who had acquired great renown for his skill in

"Marchioness of Lorne" (*built 1891*) **in Bowling Bay**

Bowling Bay in 1923

Photo. by the Author

salving stranded ships, was promptly on the spot, and succeeded in moving the steamer a matter of twenty feet, but had to desist, as she was found to be so badly holed forward that she would almost certainly have sunk when released, and before anything could be done to patch her stormy weather set in, she parted amidships, and the after portion sank. There is a curious similarity in the two strandings, and indeed the whole history of this steamer is curious, and the circumstance of her repurchase to replace the vessel which had been bought in to make good her own loss must surely be almost unique.

BY HEID-MARK

It was on board the "Columba" that I fell in with him. A man of middle height, with a short iron-grey beard; one might have guessed his age anywhere between fifty and sixty. He was dressed in a navy serge suit with no pretension to style in cut, and a black bowler hat, and in the marone tie, knotted tightly up to the throat of his turn-down collar, he wore a pin headed with a large square cairngorm in a gold setting. His hands, though not scrupulously manicured, gave no indication of connection with any of the heavy trades, and I set him down mentally as a well-to-do shopkeeper in a small way. It was as we were passing Bowling that I first noticed him, standing on the saloon-deck, abaft the paddle-box, his attention riveted on a red-funnelled paddle-steamer moored in the dock. Finding myself unable to place the steamer as belonging to the Clyde fleet, I turned to him and asked him if he knew what she was.

"Man, dae ye no' ken that yin?" he asked; "that's the 'Glencoe,' the auld 'Mary Jane'; she's mair nor seeventy year auld. She used to be on the Inveraray rin, mair nor forty year sin'; her an' the 'Inveraray Castle'; they ran day aboot. Six o'clock the ae mornin' frae the Broomielaw an' six

the next mornin' frae Inveraray. They took it gae
canny; the single trip lastet the haill day. The
baith o' them had fiddle-bows an' twa masts, but
by an' by they ta'en the 'Mary Jane' aff the rin,
an' pit a saloon in her, tae mak' a tourist steamer
o' her. They ta'en oot yin o' the masts, an' ta'en
the bowsprit an' heidboards aff her, an' ca'ed her
the 'Glencoe.' That's forty year sin', an' she's a
guid boat yet. No' mony steamers ye see noo wi'
the funnel ahint the paidle-boxes. They wis a
guid wheen o' them when A min'; the 'Balmoral,'
an' the 'Vesta,' an' the 'Hero,' an' the 'Vulcan,'
an' the 'Vale o' Clwyd,' an' the 'Dunoon Castle,'
an' the 'Petrel,' the aul' Sunday boat. Steeple-
engined maist o' them were; a' excep' the wee
'Vulcan,' A think; she had a rale bonny wee pair
o' oscillators. You'll no' hae min' o' the 'Vulcan';
she sailt for mony a day doon tae Clydebank wi'
Thomson's workers, an' a coorse lot they were!"

I had to admit that the "Vulcan" was before
my day.

"Ay, A believe she wud; it's a lang while noo
since she gaed tae the foondry. Ah weel, she wis
the only yin that had oscillators; a' the rest that
Ah wis speakin' aboot wis steeple-engined. That
auld yin we passed the noo has a steeple tae; no'
the oreeginal engine, though; she wis re-engined
no' long after they pit the saloon in her. An', man,
there's anither thing aboot her ye'll no' see often;
if ye wis alangside her ye wid see she's clinker-
built, the plates owrelappin' like a rowin'-boat;

there's nae steamers built that wey nooadays. She must hae been a gran' job tae begin wi'; it wis Tod & M'Gregor built her, sae nae doot she got the best o' material an' the best o' workmanship pit intae her."

"You said she's over seventy years old," I said. "She surely must be the oldest steamer afloat."

"Naw, man," he said, "ye're wrang. There's an aulder yin up in the canawl at Inverness, the aul' 'Glengarry'; she's seeventy-five year auld; this yin's only seeventy-three. A seen the 'Glengarry' a week or twa sin' lyin' up at Muirtoon, a' guttit oot, wi' the saloon oot her, an' yin o' the paidle-boxes aff her, an' nae hurricane-deck, juist the biler an' engine stickin' up. The engine had a tarpaulin owre't tae keep the rain aff it. A believe it's the oreeginal auld steeple that wis pit intae her when she wis built."

"Are they breaking her up?" I asked.

"Damn the fear! She's faur owre guid a pro-perty tae break up; thae auld airn boats 'll last for ever if they're ta'en care o'. Naw, naw, she's get-tin' a complete overhaul, an' A'll warrant if ye wis gaun up the canawl next spring ye wid fin' her dune up like the fute o' an aul' buit. Oh, thon yin 'll lest oot her hunner year, an' luk as fresh as pent at the en' o't."

"Did you sail down the canal?" I asked.

"Ay, A cam doon tae Banavie in the 'Gon-dolier'; she's a guid aul' boat, but no' near sae aul' as the 'Glengarry' an' the 'Mary Jane.' Nice wee pair o' oscillators thon she has; ye don't see very mony o' them noo, ayther."

"Beautiful sail up Loch Ness, isn't it?" I said. "Had you good weather?"

"Oh, it wis a wee shooery, bit, man, we passed the auld 'Sultan' when we wis jist at thon aul' castle; whit's this they ca't?"

"Urquhart Castle?" I suggested. "Very picturesque at that part, isn't it?"

"Oh, ay, it's a' that; A see they ca' her the 'Gairlochy' noo; they've shortened her a bit tae, tae gang through the locks; but, man, she luks fine wi' the red funnel, an' a' thon deck-houses; ye'll min' o' her on the Clyde?"

"She belonged to Williamson, didn't she?" I said.

"Ay, that's the boat; her an' the wee 'Sultana'; ye min' her? Man, thon wis a boat; an awfu' bonny wee model, awfu' long furrit o' the paidle-boxes, an' an awfu' fine entrance, an' thon cocky wee funnel o' hers, wi' the steam-pipe in front o't. An', man, she could fairly traivel. They tell me she yince ran frae Princes Pier tae Rothesay in fifty-seeven meenits, no' straucht owre, min' ye, but stoppin' at a' the piers."

"We haven't improved much on that yet," I remarked.

"Improved on't! Man, there's no' yin o' the boats the day could come near't, wi' a' their compound engines an' their turbines. A tell ye the boats they built forty or fifty year ago wis faur faster than the new yins."

"This is a fairly old boat we're on," I said.

"Weel, she is an' she isna; it's mair nor forty year since she was built, but it's no' like she had been sair wrocht. Min', she's never sailt mair nor three or fower months in the year, an' no' hard ca'ed at that, jist six days a week, Glesca tae Ardrishaig an' back. Sae ye micht say she's no' mair in a wey than ten year aul'. An' then, she's aye been keepit in the best o' order, an' she's as guid the day as the day she was built. A'm shair ye couldna ask onything better than this."

"She's really a very comfortable boat," I said. "Have you something to do with the Clyde steamers, that you take so deep an interest in them?"

"Naw, naw," he said, "A'm in the grocery tred; the steamers is jist a hobby wi' me, hiv been ever since A wis a laddie. Is that them checkin' the tickets? The wife's doon the stair. A'll better gang doon an' gie her hers; she'll be winderin' whit's come owre me onyway. Weel, solong the noo. A'll maybe rin across ye again by an' by."

And with that he left me. The steamers seemed to be his one interest; the old "Glengarry" and "Mary Jane" had evidently more charm for him than all the glories of Loch Ness and the canal. A simple soul, but I could find no ground to commiserate him because all the romantic history of Urquhart Castle, as retailed by the guide-book to the credulous tourist, was as nothing to him, compared to the fact that the old "Sultan" had been shortened to fit the locks on the canal.

A Corner of Bowling Bay in 1923

APPENDIX

STEAMERS PLYING IN THE CLYDE RIVER-SERVICE IN 1816.

Clyde - - - - - -	Capt. M'Kenzie.
Glasgow - - - - -	Capt. Cook.
Prince of Orange - - - -	Capt. M'Innes.
Princess Charlotte - - -	Capt. Duncan.
Britannia - - - - -	Capt. Wise.
Dumbarton Castle - - -	Capt. Thomson.
Argyle - - - - - -	Capt. Dick.
Wellington - - - - -	Capt. M'Kinley.
Waterloo - - - - -	Capt. Muirhead.
Lord Nelson - - - -	Capt. Carswell.
Rothesay Castle - - - -	Capt. Johnston.
Albion - - - - - -	Capt. Kay.
Neptune - - - - -	Capt. Leitch.

Also the " Trusty " and " Industry," cargo steamers.

STEAMERS PLYING ON THE CLYDE, ETC., ETC., from *Lumsden's Steamboat Companion*, 1820.

Comet - -	28 tons	14 H.P.	To Fort-William.
Argyle - -	78 ,,	26 ,,	,, Inveraray.
Britannia -	109 ,,	32 ,,	,, Campbeltown.
Neptune -	82 ,,	20 ,,	,, Inveraray.
Rob Roy -	87 ,,	30 ,,	,, Belfast.
Robert Bruce	150 ,,	60 ,,	,, Liverpool.
Inveraray Castle	112 ,,	40 ,,	,, Inveraray.
Superb -	240 ,,	72 ,,	,, Liverpool.
Rapid - -	136 ,,	40 ,,	,, Liverpool and Belfast.
Clyde - -	65 ,,	14 ,,	,, Ports of Clyde.
Glasgow -	64 ,,	14 ,,	,, ,,

Greenock - -	62 tons	10 H.P.	To Ports of Clyde.
Waterloo - -	90 ,,	20 ,,	,, ,,
Albion - -	92 ,,	20 ,,	,, ,,
Rothesay Castle -	95 ,,	30 ,,	,, ,,
Oscar - - -	54 ,,	12 ,,	,, ,,
Dunbarton -	65 ,,	25 ,,	,, ,,
Defiance -	51 ,,	12 ,,	,, ,,
Marquis of Bute -	53 ,,	14 ,,	,, ,,
Robert Burns -	66 ,,	20 ,,	,, ,,
Port-Glasgow -	84 ,,	16 ,,	,, ,,
Fingal - -	67 ,,	16 ,,	,, ,,
Post Boy - -	65 ,,	20 ,,	,, ,,

Also the " Samson," tug-boat, of 40 horse-power, fitted-up for passengers, belonging to the Clyde Shipping Co.

LIST OF ALL THE STEAM-VESSELS PLYING AT THE PORT OF GLASGOW IN 1828 AS RECORDED IN THE MINUTE-BOOKS OF THE CHAMBER OF COMMERCE.

Ayr - - -	75 tons	60 H.P.	To Ayr.
Albion -	69 ,,	30 ,,	,, Millport.
Countess of Glasgow -	89 ,,	45 ,,	,, Irvine.
Largs - -	83 ,,	32 ,,	,, Millport.
Britannia -	73 ,,	28 ,,	,, Londonderry.
Eclipse -	104 ,,	70 ,,	,, Belfast.
Fingal -	202 ,,	100 ,,	,, ,,
Frolic - -	99 ,,	90 ,,	,, ,,
Erin - -	207 ,,	100 ,,	,, Dublin.
Scotia - -	165 ,,	100 ,,	,, ,,
Enterprise -	125 ,,	80 ,,	,, Liverpool.
Wm. Huskisson -	227 ,,	120 ,,	,, ,,
Henry Bell -	110 ,,	60 ,,	,, ,,
James Watt	115 ,,	80 ,,	,, ,,
Solway -	192 ,,	90 ,,	,, ,,
Duke of Lancaster	91 ,,	50 ,,	,, Campbeltown.
Dumbarton Castle	81 ,,	64 ,,	,, Stranraer.

Dunoon Castle	-	79 tons	55 H.P.	To Inveraray.	
Inveraray Castle	-	70 ,,	40 ,,	,, ,,	
Rothesay Castle	-	67 ,,	55 ,,	,, Rothesay and Lamlash.	
Toward Castle	-	79 ,,	45 ,,	,, Rothesay.	
Maid of Islay	-	74 ,,	45 ,,	,, East Tarbert & Rothesay.	
George Canning	-	80 ,,	35 ,,	,, Rothesay.	
Ewing	- -	77 ,,	36 ,,	,, ,,	
Ben Nevis	- -	44 ,,	32 ,,	,, Stornoway.	
Highlander	- -	51 ,,	27 ,,	,, Staffa and Tobermory.	
Maid of Morven	-	52 ,,	32 ,,	,, Inverness.	
Highland Chieftain		51 ,,	32 ,,	,, ,,	
Caledonia	- -	57 ,,	35 ,,	,, Helensburgh.	
Waverley	- -	70 ,,	35 ,,	,, ,,	
Helensburgh	-	88 ,,	50 ,,	,, ,,	
Clarence	- -	70 ,,	45 ,,	,, ,,	
Sovereign	- -	68 ,,	32 ,,	,, ,,	
Sultan	- -	69 ,,	40 ,,	,, ,,	
Bangor Castle	-	36 ,,	30 ,,	,, Dumbarton.	
Dumbarton	- -	50 ,,	24 ,,	,, ,,	
New Dumbarton	-	72 ,,	40 ,,	,, ,,	
Leven	- - -	71 ,,	30 ,,	,, ,,	
Lady of the Lake	-	62 ,,	25 ,,	,, ,,	
Oscar	- - -	43 ,,	18 ,,	,, Gourock.	
Robert Bruce	-	48 ,,	20 ,,	,, ,,	
St. Catherine	-	73 ,,	34 ,,	,, Arrochar.	
St. George	- -	73 ,,	48 ,,	,, Lochgoilhead.	
Londonderry	-	102 ,,	74 ,,	,, Londonderry.	
Samson	- -	49 ,,	40 ,,	⎱	
Hercules	- -	74 ,,	50 ,,	⎰ Tug-boats.	
Gulliver	- -	74 ,,	60 ,,		
Active	- -	59 ,,	10 ,,	⎱	
Despatch	- -	58 ,,	10 ,,		
Industry	- -	58 ,,	10 ,,	⎰ Cargo-boats.	
Trusty	- -	61 ,,	18 ,,		
Commerce	- -	60 ,,	20 ,,		
Favourite	- -	60 ,,	20 ,,	⎰	

STEAMERS PLYING ON THE CLYDE IN 1833, as Recorded
    in Fowler's Commercial Directory of Renfrewshire
    for 1833-4.

Leven	-	54 tons to Dumbarton and Arrochar.	
Benledi	-	115 ,,	Largs, Millport, and Ayr.
Nimrod	-	96 ,,	,, ,, ,,
Antelope	-	161 ,,	Belfast.
Belfast	-	123 ,,	,,
City of Glasgow	-	183 ,,	,,
Eclipse	-	104 ,,	,,
Fingal	-	202 ,,	,,
Toward Castle	-	97 ,,	,,
Duke of Lancaster	90 ,,	Campbeltown.	
Foyle	-	136 ,,	Campbeltown and Londonderry.
Londonderry	-	102 ,,	,, ,,
St. Columb	-	140 ,,	,, ,,
Scotia	-	165 ,,	Dublin.
New Dumbarton	-	72 ,,	Dumbarton.
Active	-	59 ,,	
Alert	-	60 ,,	
Commerce	-	60 ,,	Luggage boats between Glasgow
Dispatch	-	58 ,,	and Greenock every lawful
Favourite	-	60 ,,	day.
Industry	-	55 ,,	
Trusty	-	61 ,,	
Gulliver	-	74 ,,	
Hercules	-	74 ,,	Tug-boats.
Samson	-	49 ,,	
Arran Castle	-	81 ,,	Gourock, Dunoon, and Rothesay.
Earl Grey	-	105 ,,	Gourock, Dunoon, Kilmun, and Rothesay.
Dunoon Castle	-	100 ,,	Gourock, Rothesay, and Lochgilphead.
Kilmun	-	102 ,,	Gourock, Dunoon, Kilmun, and Rothesay.

Ship	Tons		Destination
Inveraray Castle	-	70 tons to	Gourock, Rothesay, and Lochgilphead.
Windsor Castle	-	90 ,,	Gourock, Dunoon, and Rothesay.
St. Mungo -	-	63 ,,	Kilmun.
Fairy Queen	-	40 ,,	Largs and Millport.
Hero -	-	60 ,,	,, ,,
Albion	-	64 ,,	Largs, Millport, and Arran.
Largs -	-	103 ,,	Lochgilphead.
Gleniffer	-	32 ,,	Paisley and Kilmun.
Loch Ryan -	-	94 ,,	Stranraer.
St. Catherine	-	73 ,,	Lochgoilhead.
Caledonia	-	57 ,,	Helensburgh and Rosneath.
Clarence	-	70 ,,	,, ,,
Greenock -	-	70 ,,	,, ,,
Helensburgh	-	81 ,,	,, ,,
James Oswald	-	68 ,,	,, ,,
Sultan	-	68 ,,	,, ,,
Waverley -	-	55 ,,	,, ,,
Inverness -	-	43 ,,	Inverness.
Maid of Morven -		52 ,,	,,
Rob Roy	-	42 ,,	,,
Staffa -	-	46 ,,	,,
Maid of Islay	-	140 ,,	Islay, Staffa, Iona, and Skye.
Highlander -	-	51 ,,	Skye.
St. David	-	110 ,,	Newry and Dublin.
Ailsa Craig -	-	170 ,,	Liverpool.
City of Glasgow	-	183 ,,	,,
Glasgow	-	210 ,,	,,
Clyde -	-	195 ,,	,,
John Wood -	-	180 ,,	,,
Liverpool	-	200 ,,	,,
Manchester -	-	219 ,,	,,
Vulcan -	-	214 ,,	,,

Also the steamer "Euphrosyne" on Loch Lomond.

STEAMERS PLYING ON THE

	1849	50	51	52	53	54	55	56	57	58	59	60	61	62
Celt	*	*	*	*	*	*	*	*	*	*	*	*	*	*
Duke of Cornwall	*	*	*	*	*	*	*	*	*	†	†	—	—	—
Breadalbane	*	*	*	*	—	—	—	—	—	—	—	—	—	—
Dumbuck	*	*	*	—	—	—	—	—	—	—	—	—	—	—
Superb	*	—	—	—	—	—	—	—	—	—	—	—	—	—
Duchess of Argyll	*	*	*	*	*	*	—	—	—	—	—	—	—	—
Star	*	*	*	*	*	*	*	*	*	*	*	*	*	*
Lady Kelburne	*	*	*	*	*	*	*	*	*	*	*	*	*	*
Invincible	*	*	*	*	*	*	*	*	—	—	—	—	—	—
Lady Brisbane	*	*	*	*	*	*	*	*	*	*	*	*	*	*
Mars	*	*	*	*	*	*	*	—	—	—	—	—	—	—
Isle of Arran	*	*	*	*	*	*	*	*	*	*	*	—	—	—
Premier	*	*	*	*	*	*	*	*	*	*	*	—	—	—
Dumbarton Castle	*	—	—	—	—	—	—	—	—	—	—	—	—	—
Fire Queen	*	—	—	—	—	—	—	—	—	—	—	—	—	—
Mary Jane	*	*	*	*	*	*	*	*	*	*	*	*	*	*
Pioneer	*	*	*	—	—	—	—	—	—	—	—	—	—	—
Vesper	*	—	—	—	—	—	—	—	—	—	—	—	—	—
Sovereign	*	*	*	*	*	*	*	—	—	—	—	—	—	—
Monarch	*	*	*	*	*	—	—	—	—	—	—	—	—	—
Emperor ⎫ Acquilla ⎭	*	*	*	*	*	*	*	*	*	*	*	*	*	†
Prince	*	*	*	*	†	†	—	—	—	—	—	—	—	—
Dolphin	*	*	*	*	*	*	*	*	*	*	*	*	*	*
Queen	—	*	*	*	—	—	—	—	—	—	—	—	—	—
Scotia	*	*	*	*	*	*	*	*	*	*	*	*	*	*
Lochlomond	*	*	*	—	—	—	—	—	—	—	—	—	—	—
Plover	*	*	*	—	—	—	—	—	—	—	—	—	—	—
Petrel	*	*	*	*	*	*	*	*	*	*	*	*	*	*
Dunrobin Castle	*	*	*	—	—	—	—	—	—	—	—	—	—	—
Craignish Castle	*	*	*	*	*	*	*	*	*	*	*	*	*	*
Cardiff Castle	*	*	*	*	*	*	—	—	*	*	*	*	*	*
Ardentinny	—	—	*	*	*	*	—	—	—	—	—	—	—	—
Eclipse	—	—	*	*	*	*	—	—	—	—	—	—	—	—
Merlin	*	*	*	*	*	*	*	—	—	—	—	—	—	—
Pilot	*	*	*	*	—	—	—	—	—	—	—	—	—	—

CLYDE FROM 1849 TO 1869.

```
63 64 65 66 67 68 69
 *  *  *  *  †· †  —   Sent to Calcutta 1868.
 —  —  —  —  —  —  —   Auctioned 1859.   Destination unknown.
 —  —  —  —  —  —  —   Sold to Australia.
 —  —  —  —  —  —  —
 —  —  —  —  —  —  —
 —  —  —  —  —  —  —
 *  —  —  —  —  —  —   Went blockade-running.   Still afloat.
 *  *  *  *  †  †  †   Sold 1869.   Probably broken-up.
 —  —  —  —  —  —  —   Sold foreign.
 *  *  *  *  *  *  *   Re-named " Balmoral."   Converted into
                          hulk.
 —  —  —  —  —  —  —   Wrecked.
 —  —  —  —  —  —  —   Broken-up 1860.
 —  —  —  —  —  —  —   Still afloat at Weymouth.
 —  —  —  —  —  —  —
 —  —  —  —  —  —  —   Built as a yacht.
 *  *  *  *  *  *  *   Now the West Highland steamer "Glencoe."
 —  —  —  —  —  —  —   Transferred to West Highland trade.
 —  —  —  —  —  —  —
 —  —  —  —  —  —  —
 —  —  —  —  —  —  —   Sent to Tasmania 1854.
 —  —  —  —  —  —  —
 *  *  —  —  —  —  —
 —  —  —  —  —  —  —   Hull (wood) and engine sold separately
                          1855.
 —  —  —  —  —  —  —   Went blockade-running.
 —  —  —  —  —  —  —
 *  —  —  —  —  —  —   Went blockade-running.
 —  —  —  —  —  —  —
 —  —  —  —  —  —  —   Blown-up 1851.   Sold to Lancashire Ry.
 *  *  *  *  *  *  *   Broken-up about 1885.
 —  —  —  —  —  —  —   Sold to Russia.
 —  —  —  —  —  —  —   Probably went blockade-running.
 *  *  *  *  †  —  —
 —  —  —  —  —  —  —
 —  —  —  —  —  —  —   Wrecked.
 —  —  —  —  —  —  —   Damaged in 1856 storm.   Not sailing again.
 —  —  —  —  —  —  —   Sent to Belfast.
```

	1849	50	51	52	53	54	55	56	57	58	59	60	61	62
Dunoon Castle	*	*	*			*	†							
Inveraray Castle	*	*	*	*	*	*	*	*	*			*	*	*
Argyle	*	*	*	*	*	*	*	*	*	*	*	*	*	*
Argyll	*	*	*											
Ayrshire Lass	*	*	*	*	*	*	*	*	*	*	*	*	*	*
Mountaineer						*	*	*	*	*	*	*	*	*
Osprey				*	*									
Venus						*	*	*	*	*	*	*	*	*
Glasgow Citizen				*	*									
Eagle						*	*	*	*	*	*	*	*	*
Koh-i-Noor				*	*									
Helensburgh				*										
Dunoon				*										
Gourock				*										
Victoria				*	*	*	*	*	*	*				
Culloden		*	*	*										
Reindeer				*	*	*	*							
Duke of Argyll				*	*	*	*	*	†	†				
Rotatory Steamer					*									
Dumbarton						*								
Gareloch												*	*	
Chancellor					*	*	*	*	*	*	*	*	*	*
Wellington					*	*	*	*	*	*	*	*	*	*
Vesta					*	*	*	*	*					
Baron					*	*	*	*	*					
Eva				*										
Rothesay Castle (3)						*	*	*	*	*	*	*		
Ruby (1)						*	*	*	*	*	*			
Loch Goil						*	*	*	*	*	*	*	*	*
Express						*	*	*	*	*	*	*	*	*
Gem						*	*	*	*	*	*	*	*	*
Vulcan						*	*	*	*	*	*	*	*	*
Sir Colin Campbell						*	*							
Nelson						*	*	*	*	*	*	*	*	*
Alma							*	*	*	*	*	*	*	*
Iona (1)								*	*	*	*	*	*	*
Jupiter								*	*					
Mail (1)								*						
Artizan								*	*	*	*	*	*	*
Caledonia									*	*	*			
Alliance														
Druid									*	*	*	*	*	*
Royal Burgh									*	*				
Spunkie									*	*	†	†	*	*
Kelpie									*	*				

63	64	65	66	67	68	69	
—	—	—	—	—	—	—	Wooden. Sold for breaking-up 1856.
*	*	*	*	*	*	*	Broken-up about 1893.
—	—	—	—	—	—	—	Inveraray-St. Catherine's ferry.
—	—	—	—	—	—	—	Screw-steamer.
*	*	—	—	—	—	—	Sold to Japan 1864.
*	*	*	*	*	*	*	Wrecked 1889.
—	—	—	—	—	—	—	Posted as missing 1854.
*	*	*	*	*	*	*	Broken-up about 1874.
—	—	—	—	—	—	—	Went to Australia 1853. Foundered 1863.
—	—	—	—	—	—	—	Went blockade-running.
—	—	—	—	—	—	—	Went to Shannon 1853. Foundered 1855.
—	—	—	—	—	—	—	
—	—	—	—	—	—	—	
—	—	—	—	—	—	—	
—	—	—	—	—	—	—	Went to Belfast Lough 1852.
—	—	—	—	—	—	—	Went to Memel, Russia, 1855.
—	—	—	—	—	—	—	Sank in Sound of Mull 1858. Raised, but
—	—	—	—	—	—	—	not on Clyde again.
—	—	—	—	—	—	—	
*	—	—	—	—	—	—	Went blockade-running. Wrecked.
—	—	—	—	—	—	—	Broken-up 1860.
*	*	*	*	*	*	*	Burnt 1885.
—	—	—	—	—	—	—	Went to France 1857.
—	—	—	—	—	—	—	Sold to Australia. Foundered Dec. 1853.
—	—	—	—	—	—	—	Went to India.
*	*	*	*	*	*	*	Became " Lough Foyle " and " Loch Ness." Broken-up.
*	—	—	—	—	—	—	Broken-up 1865.
*	—	—	—	—	—	—	Went blockade-running.
*	*	*	*	*	*	*	Broken-up about 1880.
—	—	—	—	—	—	—	Double-bowed boat.
*	*	*	*	*	*	*	Sold to West Africa.
*	*	*	—	—	—	—	Broken-up 1865.
—	—	—	—	—	—	—	Sold for blockade. Sunk by collision.
*	—	—	—	—	—	—	Went blockade-running.
—	—	—	—	—	—	—	Sold to Russia 1857.
—	—	—	—	—	—	—	Plied between Glasgow and Rutherglen.
*	—	—	—	—	—	—	Went blockade-running.
—	—	—	—	—	—	—	Went blockade-running. Wrecked on N.Z. coast.
*	*	*	*	*	*	†	
—	—	—	—	—	—	—	Plied between Glasgow and Rutherglen.
*	—	—	—	—	—	—	Went blockade-running.
—	—	—	—	—	—	—	Went to Shannon, becoming blockade-runner.

	1849	50	51	52	53	54	55	56	57	58	59	60	61	62
Hero	-	—	—	—	—	—	—	—	—	*	*	*	—	—
Windsor Castle	-	—	—	—	—	—	—	—	—		*	—	—	—
Royal Reefer	-	—	—	—	—	—	—	—	—		*	*	*	*
Loch Long	-	—	—	—	—	—	—	—	—	*	*	*	*	*
Pearl	-	—	—	—	—	—	—	—	—		*	—	—	—
Queen of Beauty	-	—	—	—	—	—	—	—	—		—	*	*	*
Mail (2)	-	—	—	—	—	—	—	—	—			*	*	*
Juno	-	—	—	—	—	—	—	—	—		—	*	*	*
Earl of Arran	-	—	—	—	—	—	—	—	—			*		
Ruby (2)	-	—	—	—	—	—	—	—	—		*	*	—	
Dumbarton (2)	-	—	—	—	—	—	—	—	—			—	*	*
Ruby (3)	-	—	—	—	—	—	—	—	—			—	*	*
Rothesay Castle (4)	—	—	—	—	—	—	—	—	—			—	*	*
Neptune	-	—	—	—	—	—	—	—	—			—	*	*
Sultan	-	—	—	—	—	—	—	—	—			—		
Iona (2)	-	—	—	—	—	—	—	—	—	—	—	—	—	—
Victory	-	—	—	—	—	—	—	—	—	—	—	—	—	—
Kilmun	-	—	—	—	—	—	—	—	—	—	—	—	—	—
Leven	-	—	—	—	—	—	—	—	—	—	—	—	—	—
Lennox	-	—	—	—	—	—	—	—	—	—	—	—	—	—
Iona (3)	-	—	—	—	—	—	—	—	—	—	—	—	—	—
Eagle (2)	-	—	—	—	—	—	—	—	—	—	—	—	—	—
Vivid	-	—	—	—	—	—	—	—	—	—	—	—	—	—
Chancellor (2)	-	—	—	—	—	—	—	—	—	—	—	—	—	—
Arran Castle	-	—	—	—	—	—	—	—	—	—	—	—	—	—
Largs	-	—	—	—	—	—	—	—	—	—	—	—	—	—
Kyles	-	—	—	—	—	—	—	—	—	—	—	—	—	—
Bute	-	—	—	—	—	—	—	—	—	—	—	—	—	—
Undine	-	—	—	—	—	—	—	—	—	—	—	—	—	—
Fairy	-	—	—	—	—	—	—	—	—	—	—	—	—	—
Rothesay Castle (5)	—	—	—	—	—	—	—	—	—	—	—	—	—	—
Argyle	-	—	—	—	—	—	—	—	—	—	—	—	—	—
Athole	-	—	—	—	—	—	—	—	—	—	—	—	—	—
Ardencaple	-	—	—	—	—	—	—	—	—	—	—	—	—	—
Rosneath	-	—	—	—	—	—	—	—	—	—	—	—	—	—
Herald	-	—	—	—	—	—	—	—	—	—	—	—	—	—
Leven	-	—	—	—	—	—	—	—	—	—	—	—	—	—
Meg Merrilies	-	—	—	—	—	—	—	—	—	—	—	—	—	—
Chevalier	-	—	—	—	—	—	—	—	—	—	—	—	—	—
Ardgowan	-	—	—	—	—	—	—	—	—	—	—	—	—	—
Dandie Dinmont	-	—	—	—	—	—	—	—	—	—	—	—	—	—
Vesper	-	—	—	—	—	—	—	—	—	—	—	—	—	—
Vale of Clwyd	-	—	—	—	—	—	—	—	—	—	—	—	—	—

63	64	65	66	67	68	69	
*	*	*	*	*	*	*	Re-named "Mountaineer." Broken-up about 1907.
—	—	—	—	—	—	—	Sold to India. Wrecked 1860.
—	—	—	—	—	—	—	Plied between Glasgow and Rutherglen.
*	*	*	*	*	*	—	
—	—	—	—	—	—	—	Went blockade-running.
—	—	—	—	—	—	—	On Greenock-Helensburgh ferry service.
*	—	—	—	—	—	—	Went blockade-running.
*	—	—	—	—	—	—	Went blockade-running.
*	*	*	*	*	*	†	
—	—	—	—	—	—	—	Sold to India. Wrecked 1860.
—	—	—	—	—	—	—	
—	—	—	—	—	—	—	Went blockade-running.
*	—	—	—	—	—	—	Went blockade-running.
—	—	—	—	—	—	—	Went blockade-running.
*	*	*	*	*	*	*	Became "Ardmore" and "Gairlochy." Burnt 1919.
*	—	—	—	—	—	—	Sold for blockade. Foundered 1864.
*	*	*	*	*	*	*	Became "Marquis of Lorne" and "Cumbrae." Hulk.
*	†	†	—	—	—	—	Stern-wheeler. Only ran one week.
—	*	*	*	—	—	—	Sold to Brazil. Wrecked 1867.
—	*	*	*	—	—	—	Sold to Brazil. Wrecked 1867.
—	*	*	*	*	*	*	Still plying on the Firth.
—	*	*	*	*	*	*	Sent to Manchester 1894. Broken-up 1895
—	*	*	*	*	*	*	Broken-up 1902.
—	*	*	*	*	*	*	Became "Shandon" and "Daniel Adamson." Broken-up 1895.
—	*	*	*	—	—	—	Left for Thames, 1866. Posted as missing.
—	—	*	*	*	*	*	Sold to Waterford 1876.
—	—	*	—	—	—	—	Sold to Thames 1866.
—	—	*	—	—	—	—	Sold to Thames 1866. Sunk by collision 1878.
—	—	*	*	*	*	*	Sold foreign 1878.
—	—	*	*	*	*	*	On Inveraray-St. Catherine's ferry.
—	—	*	*	*	*	*	Sold to France 1878.
—	—	—	*	*	*	*	Went to Tay 1890.
—	—	—	*	*	*	*	Broken-up about 1893.
—	—	—	*	*	*	*	Went to Thames 1875.
—	—	—	*	*	*	*	Went to Waterford 1871.
—	—	—	*	—	—	—	Went to Barrow for Isle of Man trade.
—	—	—	*	*	*	*	Went to the Thames 1875.
—	—	—	*	†	—	—	Went to the Forth 1868.
—	—	—	*	*	*	*	Still afloat, plying occasionally on Clyde.
—	—	—	*	*	*	*	Went to the Thames 1875.
—	—	—	*	†	†	*	Went to South of England 1888.
—	—	—	*	—	—	—	Sold to Brazil. Wrecked 1867.
—	—	—	*	*	*	*	Went to the Thames 1881.

	1849	50	51	52	53	54	55	56	57	58	59	60	61	62
Vale of Doon	-	—	—	—	—	—	—	—	—	—	—	—	—	—
Gael - -	-	—	—	—	—	—	—	—	—	—	—	—	—	—
Elaine - -	-	—	—	—	—	—	—	—	—	—	—	—	—	—
Dunoon Castle	-	—	—	—	—	—	—	—	—	—	—	—	—	—
Loch Lomond	-	—	—	—	—	—	—	—	—	—	—	—	—	—
Lancelot -	-	—	—	—	—	—	—	—	—	—	—	—	—	—
Sultana -	-	—	—	—	—	—	—	—	—	—	—	—	—	—
Marquis of Bute	-	—	—	—	—	—	—	—	—	—	—	—	—	—
The Lady Mary	-	—	—	—	—	—	—	—	—	—	—	—	—	—
Kintyre -	-	—	—	—	—	—	—	—	—	—	—	—	—	—
Guinevere -	-	—	—	—	—	—	—	—	—	—	—	—	—	—
Carham -	-	—	—	—	—	—	—	—	—	—	—	—	—	—

* Signifies that the steamer was plying on
† Signifies that the steamer was laid up on

63	64	65	66	67	68	69	
—	—	—	*	*	—	—	Went to South America 1868.
—	—	—	—	*	*	*	Still afloat in West Highland trade.
—	—	—	—	*	*	*	Broken-up 1899.
—	—	—	—	*	*	*	Went to the Mersey 1890.
—	—	—	—	*	*	†	
—	—	—	—	—	*	*	Sold to Constantinople 1890.
—	—	—	—	—	*	*	Sold to France about 1899.
—	—	—	—	—	*	*	Went to North of England about 1908.
—	—	—	—	—	*	*	Went to Bristol Channel 1874.
—	—	—	—	—	*	*	Sunk by collision 1907.
—	—	—	—	—	—	*	Sold to Constantinople. Foundered about 1892.
—	—	—	—	—	—	*	In North British Co.'s Gareloch and Dunoon services.

the Clyde in the year indicated.

the Clyde in the year indicated, but not plying.

GENERAL INDEX

Advertisements, 38, 39, 45, 46, 47, 48, 49, 50, 61.
Ailsa Craig, Excursion to, 42.
Arran, Inaccessibility of, 37.
Ayr, Excursion to, 42, 43.

Barr & M'Nab, 103.
Barrie, Captain, 77.
Belfast, Day Excursion to, 43.
Belfast Trade started, 24.
Bell, Henry, 7, 12, 13, 22, 27.
Blackwood & Gordon, 133, 134.
Blockade-runners, 52, 53, 86, 101, 127-8, 129-143, 146, 163.
Bowling Bay, 82-6.
Bridgewater, Duke of, 11.
Brown, Capt. Charlie, 113, 122, 127.
Buchanan Steamers, 83.
Burns, G. & J., 55, 131, 132, 135.
Burns, John, 148.

Cabin furnishing, 12, 15, 17, 58-9, 89.
Caird & Co., 19, 110, 119, 134, 135, 146, 163, 164.
Caledonian Canal, 28, 56, 101, 173.
Caledonian Steamers, 82, 153.
Cameron, T., & Co., 133, 140.
Campbell & Gillies, 79, 153.
Campbell, Capt. Malcolm, 112.
Campbell, Capt. Robert, 135.
Caravans, 1, 5.
Castle Company, 61, 76.
Clyde Improved Steamboat Co., Ltd., 97, 100.

Clyde Shipping Co., 19, 134, 159.
Coaches, 1, 25, 38.
Cochrane, Mr. (Tanner), 19.
Collisions, 29, 35, 91, 106, 132, 152, 165, 166, 167.
Colquhoun, Sir James, 63-7.
Connell, Charles, & Co., 135.
Coppin, Captain, 168.
Crinan Canal, 28, 55, 56.

Deck Saloons, 39, 98, 140, 146, 159.
Delaware, Steamboat on the, 9.
Denny, Wm., & Bros., 23, 34, 131, 132.
Dobbie, George, 19.
Douglas, Capt. William, 13.
Dover and Calais Trade started, 24.
Dublin & Glasgow Steam Packet Co., 134, 163, 167.
Duncan, Robert, & Co., 165.
Dunoon, 4.

"Emperor of China," 130.
Engines, 10, 20, 22, 30, 32, 69, 70, 74, 77, 80, 84, 95, 111, 119, 146, 166, 172, 173, 174.
Explosions, 30, 31, 32, 34.

Fares, 18, 38, 43, 57, 62, 70, 72, 76, 91, 101, 152.
Ferry-boat accidents, 35-6.
Fires on board, 30, 52.
Fitch, John, 9.
Fly-boats, 2, 3.

Forth & Clyde Canal, Steamboats on, 10, 11.
Frost of 1855, 86.
Frost, Captain, 116.
Fulda, Steamboat on the, 8.
Fulton, Robert, 11, 12.
Funnels fitted for sail-carrying, 13, 17.
Furnace-bars, Hollow, 71, 73.
Fyfe, William, 19.

Garay, Blasco de, 8.
Gareloch Piers barricaded, 64, 66.
Gillies, Capt. Alex., 52.
"Glasgow Courier," 13.
"Glasgow Herald," 45, 46, 47, 120, 126, 164.
"Glasgow Monthly Repository," 16, 17, 18.
Glasgow & South Western Steamers, 82.
Gonzalez, Thomas, 8.
Greenock Harbour, 82.
Hand-paddle Boats, 8, 12.
Harland & Wolff, 166.
Hedderwick & Co., 36.
Hedderwick, Mr. (Shipbuilder), 31.
Henderson, James, & Sons, 110, 119, 132, 136.
Henderson, J. M'Clintock, 119.
Hill, Laurence, & Co., 133.
Holiday Sailings, 34-5, 43, 46, 56, 99.
Hudson, Steamer on the, 12.
Hulls, Jonathan, 9.
Hurricane of 1856, 85.
Hutcheson, David, & Co., 55, 133, 140.
Hutcheson, Master David, 57.

Inch Tavannach, View from, 39.
"Irish Times," 165.

Keith, Hugh, 52.
Kelvingrove Art Galleries, 22.

Lancashire and Furness Railway, 34.
Largs, 5.
Largs and Millport Sailings, 45, 46.
Lincoln, President, 129.
Liquor on Sunday Steamers, 105.
Liverpool Trade started, 24.
Loch Katrine Sailings, 41.
Loch Lomond Steamers, 23, 25, 38.
Loch Long–Loch Lomond Route, 40.
Londonderry Trade started, 24.
Lord Provost of Glasgow, 76.
Lumsden's "Steamboat Companion," 25, 37.

MacBrayne, David, Ltd., 55.
M'Connell & Laird, 133.
M'Gregor, D. (Steward), 38-9, 41.
M'Gregor, John, 8.
M'Innes, Duncan, 13.
M'Intyre, Captain, 127.
M'Kellar, Capt. Duncan, 45, 153.
M'Kellar's Boats, 45, 51, 52, 134, 137, 145, 147.
M'Kenzie, Capt. William, 13.
M'Lean, Capt. Sandy, 125, 126.
Miller, Patrick, 10.
Millport Sailings (see Largs).
Mills, George, 96, 137.

Napier, David, 12, 18, 23, 25, 32, 70.
Napier, Robt., & Sons, 119, 163.
Narrow escape of "Emperor," 63.
North British Steamers, 83.

Oar-propelled Steamboat, 9.
Oldest steamer in the world, 20, 173.

Papin, Denis, 8.

Police Courts, 96, 108, 122, 126, 127.

Potter, Lewis, & Co., 131.

Price, Capt. Richard, 110, 113, 123, 125, 126, 127.

Protests against Sunday Steamer, 62.

Provost and Magistrates of Rutherglen, 90, 92.

Racing, 121, 122-7.

Rankin & Blackmore, 165, 166.

Report on "Lady Brisbane," 49.

Robertson, John, 12, 13, 23.

Robertson (engineer of "Comet"), 13.

Rothesay, 4.

Rowing on the Clyde, 90.

"Royal George" Coach, 1.

Running the Lights, 57, 59, 114, 128, 139, 149, 158.

Rutherglen Shipyard, 87-8.

Rutherglen Steamers, 87-93.

St. Colm's Fair, 5.

Scuffle at Garelochhead, 65.

Seath, T. B., 87, 89, 91, 93.

Simons, Wm., & Co., 119.

South American Trade, 130.

South Kensington Museum, 22.

Speed of Steamers, 17, 18, 30, 57, 59, 72, 89, 98, 109, 113, 116, 122, 123, 125, 128, 139, 158, 163, 164, 166, 168, 174.

Steam-ferries introduced, 36.

Steel Steamer, 112.

Stern-wheel Steamboats, 10, 18.

Stewart, Capt. Duncan, 150, 152.

Strandings and Sinkings, 20, 22, 23, 24, 35, 51, 60, 75-80, 102, 140, 156, 157, 159, 161, 162, 166, 168.

Sunday Steamers, 61-7, 100, 104.

Symington, William, 10.

Thames, first Steamer on the, 19.

Thomson, J. & G., 57, 131, 133, 140.

Thomson, John, 12, 15.

Tod & M'Gregor, 97, 133, 135, 137, 173.

Track-boats, 55.

Turbine Steamers, 69, 82.

Up-river Steamboats, 87-93.

Walker, Captain, 115.

Watson, Captain, 158.

Wemyss Bay Railway, 145, 153.

Wemyss Bay Route, 52, 151.

Wemyss Bay Steamboat Co., 79, 146, 148, 153, 158.

West Highland Sailings, 21, 28, 55, 56.

Wingate, Thos., & Co., 32, 146.

Wood, John, 12.

Wrecks (see Strandings, Explosions, Collisions, etc.).

Wylie & Lochhead, 22.

INDEX TO STEAMERS

Active, 23.
Adela (Channel Steamer), 130, 131, 134, 138.
Adela (River Steamer), 80.
Albert Edward, 152.
Albion, 20.
Alliance, 97-102, 137, 142.
Antona, 132, 133, 134.
Argyle, 80, 152, 153.
Argyll (1), 20, 22.
Argyll (2), 30.
Arran Castle, 158-160.
Artizan, 88-92.
Athole, 84, 126.
Ayr, 28-9.

Balmoral, 52, 172.
Baron, 136.
Bonnie Doon, 88.
Breadalbane, 155, 156.
Britannia, 20, 24.
Bute, 151.

Caledonia, 20, 22.
Caledonia (Ayr Boat), 138, 142.
Cardiff Castle, 43.
Catherine, 12.
Chancellor (1), 85, 142.
Chanticleer, 132,
Charlotte Dundas, 10, 11, 12, 69.
Cherokee, 142.
Clermont, 12.
Clyde, 16, 17.
Columba, 83, 111, 171, 175.
Comet (1), 7, 10, 12, 13, 14, 15, 21, 23, 25, 69.
Comet (2), 27-9.
Countess of Eglinton, 51, 75.
Craignish Castle, 142.

Curlew, 55.
Cygnet, 56.

Defiance, 23.
Diamond, 136, 141.
Dispatch, 23.
Dolphin, 55, 132, 141.
Duke of Argyll, 19.
Duke of Edinburgh, 168
Duke of Wellington, 23.
Dumbarton, 73, 74.
Dumbarton Castle, 20.
Dunoon Castle, 172.

Eagle (1), 85, 86, 132, 135, 140, 141.
Earl of Carlisle, 164, 165.
Earl of Dublin, 165, 166, 167.
Earl Grey, 30.
Eclipse, 75-80.
Elaine, 84.
Elizabeth, 15-17.
Emma Hendry, 142.
Emperor, 62, 63-7, 104.
Engineer, 43.
Eva, 156.

Fairy, 140, 142.
Falcon, 115.
Fingal (paddle), 25.
Fingal (screw), 132, 133.
Firefly, 43.
Fox, 135.

Gairlochy, 174.
Gareloch, 74.
Gem, 136, 142.
Giraffe, 132, 133, 134, 138, 140.
Glasgow, 16.

Glasgow Citizen, 156.
Glencoe, 171, 172.
Glengarry, 173, 174, 175.
Glow-worm, 85.
Gondolier, 173.
Great Northern, 167.
Greenock, 20.
Guinevere, 161-2.
Guy Fawkes, 165.

Hattie, 146, 147.
Havelock, 132,133,140,142,163.
Henri IV., 24.
Herald, 130, 131, 133, 137, 140.
   163.
Hero, 45.
Hero (of 1858), 135, 143, 172.

Industry, 19, 20, 23, 85.
Inveraray Castle (1), 25.
Inveraray Castle (3), 35, 80,
   84, 171.
Invincible, 51, 85.
Iona (1), 59, 109, 131-2, 158.
Iona (2), 139, 140, 158.
Iona (3), 83, 146.
Isle of Arran, 88.

Jasper, 159.
Juno, 51, 52, 53, 134, 135, 137,
   141.
Jupiter, 51,52,53,135,136,137.

Kelpie, 135.
Kenilworth, 83.
Kilmun (paddle), 35.
Kilmun (sternwheel), 18.
King Edward, 69, 70.
Kintyre, 29.
Koh-i-Noor, 157.
Kyles, 147, 149, 151, 152.

Lady Brisbane, 42, 46, 47, 48,
   49, 50, 52.
Lady Gertrude, 79, 80.
Lady Kelburne, 50, 52, 148.
Lapwing, 56.
Largs, 147, 148, 150, 151, 153.

Lennox, 160, 161.
Leopard, 130, 131, 134, 140.
Leven, 160, 161.
Lochgoil, 35.
Loch Lomond, 38-41.
Lord Clyde (1), 134, 140, 141,
   163, 164.
Lord Clyde (2), 164.
Lord Gough, 164, 165, 167.
Lucy Ashton, 88.
Lynx, 143.

Maid of Perth (track boat), 55.
Mail, 135, 137.
Marchioness of Lorne, 83.
Marion, 20, 23, 25, 38.
Marjory, 19.
Marmion, 83.
Marquis of Abercorn, 167.
Marquis of Bute, 23.
Marquis of Bute (of 1868), 126.
Mars, 51, 77, 78, 79, 80.
Mary Anne, 135.
Mary Jane, 171, 172, 174, 175.
Merlin, 76, 85, 86.
Morning Star, 19.
Mountaineer, 57-60, 109.

Nelson, 77, 88.
Neptune, 119, 120, 121, 125-8,
   133, 137.
New Zealand, 102.
Normandie, 136.

Oscar, 23.
Osprey, 157.

Pearl, 111, 112, 113, 116, 123,
   131, 134.
Petrel, 103-8, 172.
Pioneer, 55, 56, 57.
Plover, 32-4.
Post-Boy, 25, 38.
Princess Alice, 151.
Princess Charlotte, 19.
Princess Royal, 132, 133, 134.

Raven, 168.

Reindeer, 61.
Rob Roy, 23, 24.
Rob Roy (on Loch Katrine), 41.
Robert Bruce, 24.
Robert Burns, 25.
Robert E. Lee, 138.
Roe, 135.
Rotary Steamer, 70-4.
Rothesay Castle (1), 20, 22, 23.
Rothesay Castle (3), 110, 111, 112, 113, 114, 116, 119.
Rothesay Castle(4), 117, 119-28, 135, 136, 137, 140, 141, 158.
Royal Burgh, 92.
Royal Reefer, 92.
Ruby (1), 110, 111, 112, 113.
Ruby (2), 113, 116, 117, 119, 158.
Ruby (3), 117, 119-28, 132, 133, 140.
Ruby (ex Dolphin), 141.

Samson, 25.
Scotia, 136, 140, 141.
Shandon, 55, 57.
Soane, 116.
Southern Belle, 128.
Spunkie, 135, 138, 140.
Star, 51, 52, 53, 137, 140, 141.
Sultan, 174, 176.
Sultana, 174.

Sunbeam (track-boat), 55.
Superb, 43.

Talisman, 83.
Telegraph, 30-32, 47.
Thistle (paddle), 140, 142.
Thistle (screw), 132, 133, 134, 142.
Trusty, 19, 20, 23.
Tubal Cain, 132, 133, 134.
Tuskar, 134.

Vale of Clwyd, 88, 172.
Vale of Doon, 88.
Vanguard, 163, 164.
Venus, 51, 52, 85, 148, 153.
Vesper, 160-1.
Vesta, 51, 52, 143, 172.
Victor, 45, 47, 48, 49, 50, 51.
Victory, 150, 151, 152, 153.
Vulcan, 119, 143, 172.

Warrior, 45, 46.
Waterwitch, 38, 39, 41.
Waverley (1), 13.
Waverley (3), 83.
Wellington, 76, 77, 85.
Windsor Castle (of 1859), 79, 112-116, 119, 157.
Windsor Castle (of 1875), 88.
Woodford, 23.